Start Your Own

ONLINE COUPON OR DAILY DEAL BUSINESS

Additional titles in *Entrepreneur's* Startup Series

Start Your Own

Entrepreneur
MAGAZINE'S

startup

Start Your Own

ONLINE COUPON OR DAILY DEAL BUSINESS

Your Step-by-Step Guide to Success

Entrepreneur Press and Rich Mintzer

EP
Entrepreneur
PRESS®

Entrepreneur Press, Publisher
Cover Design: Beth Hansen-Winter
Production and Composition: Eliot House Productions

This publication is designed to provide accurate and authoritative information in regard to
the subject matter covered. It is sold with the understanding that the publisher is not engaged
in rendering legal, accounting or other professional services. If legal advice or other expert
assistance is required, the services of a competent professional person should be sought.

Library of Congress Cataloging-in-Publication Data
   Mintzer, Richard.
     Start your own online coupon or daily deal business/by Entrepreneur Press and Rich
Mintzer.
      p.   cm.
   Includes index.
   ISBN-13: 978-1-59918-512-5 (alk. paper)
   ISBN–10: 1-59918-512-1 (alk. paper)
     1. Coupons (Retail trade) 2. Internet marketing. 3. New business enterprises.
   I. Entrepreneur Press. II. Title.
  HF6127.M56 2013
  658.8'2—dc23   2013004435

Printed in the United States of America

17 16 15 14 13   10 9 8 7 6 5 4 3 2 1

Contents

Chapter 4

Boring Business Basics: Getting Your Business Started 53

Chapter 5

The Home Office or the Business Office 69

Chapter 8

Chapter 9

Appendix
Online Coupon and Daily Deal Resources 163

Acknowledgments

I would like to thank Mike Ludlum for giving me the opportunity to write this book and Karen Billipp for her fabulous editing and her usual support. I'd also like to thank Darrell Ellens, an expert on the daily deal industry and a very helpful gentleman.

In addition, thank you to Bona, VP of Partnership Marketing at Access Development; Marc Horne, co-creator of Daily Deal Builder; David Teichner, CEO of Yowza!!; Darin Gislon, CEO of Savvi; Michael Fairbrother, CEO of Moonlight Meadery in Londonderry, New Hampshire; Barbara Antes, owner of Westchester Ballroom in Mount Kisco, New York; Jeff Langone, owner of Witch

City Segway Tours in Salem, Massachusetts; and Brent Dedmon of FotoCabina in Orange County, California.

And finally, thank you to Dave Lipschitz and Jennifer Lipschitz, consultants and tutors in Excel; and Courtney Thurman, Startup Evangelist and Marketing Agency Founder, for their help on this book.

Preface

Two things that people seem to care very much about are saving money and spending time on the internet. As a business owner, by combining the two, you have a very good chance of success.

Of course it takes hard work to launch an online business and make it work. Business owners need to have the time commitment to start and grow their companies, including those that are strictly online.

The coupon and daily deal industries are extremely popular these days. The TV program *Extreme Couponing* on the TLC network, and the high-profile and visibility of websites such as Groupon and LivingSocial, have led the way to a new generation of people looking to find the best deals and save money. Not only that, but many of us enjoy sharing our great finds with others.

Coupon website owners, while not very outspoken nor, in some cases, transparent, manage to load up pages of manufacturers' coupons to provide consumers with discounts at their favorite grocery stores. The owners of coupon websites range from stay-at-home moms who love finding a good deal to business owners who for years worked long and hard to produce coupon books or circulars. Since coupons have been around for many years, and the idea of offering them isn't new, just the means of delivering them to the consumers.

The daily deal websites are an offshoot of "shopping clubs," only they are literally delivering deals to consumers through email and websites on a daily basis, hence the name. This rapidly growing industry is replete with business owners and merchants who are excited about providing win-win situations that deals can produce for all parties involved: customers, merchants, and you, the daily deal site owner. In essence, this would make it a win-win-win situation.

For an ethical, hard-working, passionate business owner, either a coupon or daily deal business can be lucrative. It can provide either a full-time or part-time income, depending on your time and monetary commitment, which does not need to be a lot of money. One of the best things about taking on such an online business is that start-up costs, and even operational costs, do not need to be very high, especially if you, like hundreds of thousands of business owners, elect to start off from the comfort of your own home.

This book will provide the basics for starting a business in general. It will also provide information about the coupon and daily deal industries as well as many of the specifics you will need to know to run such a business. There are a lot of variables, such as how you will differentiate yourself from your competitors and how you will market your website. These, and many other areas of business, are discussed in the upcoming pages.

If you like saving money and passing on discounts and savings to your friends and family, you will likely be a great candidate to start either a coupon or daily deal business.

So enjoy reading, and I wish you great success if you take the plunge and launch your money-saving business.

What Is the Coupon, and Daily Deal Business, All About?

Online coupons and daily deals are among the hottest trends in recent years. The overriding theme of these hot new businesses is saving money, and that is a big hit with consumers. It is also a way of drawing new business to all sorts of new establishments, from spas to restaurants to yoga classes. Both coupon and daily deal websites, in their own ways, are serving the role of bringing merchants and customers together.

In this opening chapter we'll take a look at some of the basics of the coupon and daily deal industries, such as:

- The overall industry
- The newfound popularity
- The history of coupons and daily deals
- The three types of online discount website
- Finding your niche
- Merchants and costumers

The Overall Industry

Every day, several million people find the latest emails in their inboxes from places like LivingSocial, Groupon, or another of the many daily deal websites featuring discounts on all sorts of goods and services. In addition, millions of other cost-conscious consumers make a daily or weekly pilgrimage to find online coupons before they go shopping. Technically speaking, the daily deal and coupon industries are separate, yet their goals are similar, saving consumers money.

The recent success of the daily deal sites has been generating a lot of attention. In fact, led by Groupon, with over $1.2 billion in gross revenue, and LivingSocial, with $600 million (2011 numbers), the daily deal online coupon industry is booming. Other major staples of the internet, including social media sites such as Facebook, with its "Deals," and search engines like Google, with its "Offers," are adding to the mix of locations where millions of people are getting discounts. Meanwhile, the coupon industry is also going strong with websites including: coolsavings.com, save. com, coupons.com, couponmountain.com, couponcabin.com, coupons.smartsource. com, couponmom.com, ultimatecoupons.com, mycoupons.com, hotcouponworld. com, savings.com, and many more. There are also many new daily deal and coupon sites popping up on a regular basis, which indicates the industry is not yet saturated, but in fact, still growing.

What motivates these entrepreneurs is the passion with which the American consumer has taken to this new money-saving trend. Estimates show that more than 92 million adults used online coupons or daily deals in 2012, and that number is expected to close in on 100 million in 2013.

The Newfound Popularity

Since 2009, finding discounts has become all the rage, but why? It's a combination of several key factors. First, in an unsteady economic environment, everyone is looking for a deal, be it a "daily deal" for a vacation, or a coupon to save money on the necessities at the grocery store. Families are looking more closely at their budgets and trying to make ends meet, which is increasingly difficult as employers hold back on raises or commissions, cut back on hours, or lay off employees in favor of sending jobs overseas. Tightening the money belt has become the trend of a nation "stressed out" by weak economic numbers.

Smart Tip

Tip...

Before entering the online coupon or daily deal arena as an entrepreneur, it's advantageous to become a customer by signing up with a variety of these websites. Read the emails, study their offers, use a few, and if possible, talk to some of the merchants providing the coupons or deals and find out if the process has been working out as anticipated. Are the coupons or daily deals helping their businesses?

The second reason for the latest surge in coupon and deal users is the new technology. No longer does one need to sift through pages with a scissors at the ready. Instead, savings-conscious consumers are receiving emails with offers and can easily search their favorite sites quickly and effectively by clicking to narrow down and zero in on their items of choice. In fact, with apps, buyers can find savings on their iPhones, Androids, or other mobile devices wherever they are. Vacationers can find weekly getaways and diners can find deals on restaurants of their choosing offering foods to suit the desired price range. Printing out a coupon or voucher is simple, and in some cases, redeeming by swiping your phone is even easier. The accessibility of deals and coupons in your inbox or on apps, thanks to modern technology, is bringing them to a larger market than ever before.

Stat Fact

Yes, people are coupon crazed! It is estimated that 74 percent of consumers search multiple coupon sources each week, with 25 percent spending up to an hour shopping for the best online deals.

The third reason why online coupons and daily deals have become such a major aspect of modern consumerism is the need for retailers to stay afloat in an extremely competitive environment. For merchants, attracting new customers through advertising can be costly, but presenting attractive discounts can jump-start a business in a more cost-effective manner. Coupons and deals can be used to draw customers, and their listings in emails and on the coupon/daily deal sites also serves as a means of free advertising. Of course, business owners need to know how to utilize such discounts effectively, which will be discussed later, but it's safe to say that done correctly, a struggling business can get back on a profitable course through the use of deals and coupons without spending a fortune on advertising.

The History of Coupons: They're Not New

The popularity of coupons is not entirely new. Coupons in America are generally traced back to 1887, a year after the first appearance of Coca-Cola syrup in an Atlanta drugstore. A partner in the young Coca-Cola Company, Asa Candler, came up with the idea of mailing complimentary coupons for Coca-Cola to potential customers, while also placing them in magazines. To cover the cost savings of the coupons, Coca-Cola gave free syrup to local soda fountains. The plan worked. Over the span of 25 years, Coca-Cola gave out 8.5 million free sodas, and as a result people fell in love with the product. By 1919, the Coca-Cola Company was sold for $25 million, proving that those free introductory coupons worked.

It was also in the early 20th century that C. W. Post conceived the idea of using coupons to help sell breakfast cereals and other products. Their one-cent coupons on Grape Nuts breakfast cereals may not sound like much today, but at the time the promotion drew millions of customers.

Following the stock market crash of 1929, with the start of the Great Depression, coupons became much more widely used. Many families seeking any kind of savings became avid coupon clippers. These were not savings on extravagant spas and vacations that are offered today, but good old coupons for the bare necessities (also offered today) that were so hard to afford, such as milk, bread, and warm clothing. A few pennies off were a great savings for most Americans who were struggling at the time. Meanwhile, the storeowners were happy to have the business even if they were not making as much as they had in the past. They were trying hard to stay in business. The public had needs, and the storeowners who could fulfill those needs with the best prices stood to survive. It was during the 1930s that many people became familiar with cutting coupons at an early age and continued that activity for many years to come, often passing it on to the next generation.

During World War II, a different type of coupons was issued by the government for rationing programs to limit the amount of products people could purchase. Since many companies were busily making supplies for the war, the amount of available goods in the nation was limited. As a result, families had coupons to give store retailers for products ranging from sugar to gasoline, all of which were rationed. Items that were not rationed were in some cases sold by retailers that provided discounts and coupons to get more business. It was a trying time for Americans, but business owners did what they felt was necessary to help people along during these stressful years.

By the 1950s, '60s, and even the '70s, manufacturer coupons for discounts on products such as Cheer detergent in a box, Dial soap, Ajax cleanser, Teem soft drinks, Maxwell House coffee, and many other popular goods became standard. Cutting the cardboard coupon off of a box of cereal for a discount was not at all unusual. And popular TV characters, such as Granny (Irene Ryan) from the *Beverly Hillbillies*, would be pictured on the coupon, making money of course off the endorsement while providing a friendly face to help sell the product.

The new, large chain supermarkets that emerged in the post-WWII era, along with other major retailers, also saw the advantage of coupons. Since they were now able to buy goods in major quantities, which saved them money, they could charge a little less on items to increase traffic in their stores. This drew business away from the smaller groceries who typically could not match their prices. Movie theaters used coupons to sell more popcorn and other business owners saw coupons as a way to draw customers into their establishments. Coupons became a significant part of American culture during these decades, as evidenced by statistics showing that half of all American families were cutting coupons as of 1965.

By the 1990s, however, the coupon culture had all but diminished. The economy throughout most of the decade was strong and people became less interested in spending their time looking for bargains. From 1992 until 2009, the coupon industry was relatively quiet. However, following the economic collapse of 2008, the industry, thanks largely to the internet, re-emerged, stronger than ever. Even the U.S. government used coupons to promote converter box sales for the digital TV transition. Inmar, an international marketing company, indicates that as of 2009, coupon redemptions grew by 27 percent as Americans sought out ways to curb their household expenses and get more bang for their buck. And they could do it all online! In fact, internet redemption growth skyrocketed by rising 263 percent in 2009.

Fun Fact

Ironically, those who never used their coupons from the '50s, '60s, and '70s, and for some odd reason have them saved somewhere in their attic, can still benefit from them as they are being sold today on auction sites such as eBay, some for as much as $20 each. While selling current coupons is illegal, the jury is still out on selling long expired coupons as collectibles.

Stat Fact

According to MakeLifeEasy.com, more than 3,000 manufacturers offer nearly 330 billion coupons every year—worth about $280 billion. Consumers redeem only about 8 billion of those coupons, or about $4.7 billion worth.

The coupon industry continues to generate billions of dollars with extreme couponers leading the charge.

Daily Deal History

As for the history of the daily deal industry, it's fairly new, based in part on the old "buy now while supplies last" approach of TV advertising dating back to the 1950s. The shopping channels of the 1990s also offered deals if you acted quickly. But it wasn't until the internet age that the deal concept that we know today began. A European company named Vente-Privée was among the first to form a private shopping club in 2001. The company offered luxury brands, which combined exclusivity with a time-limited event. They gained 5 million members over the next six years. This was the beginning of online private sales.

Meanwhile, in 2004, a website called Woot.com began the concept of offering daily deals on various products. But it wasn't until 2006 that daily deal sites started appearing on a regular basis, with more than 100 popping up that year alone. With LivingSocial appearing in 2007 and Groupon in 2008, coupled with MySpace and Facebook leading the way in connecting the masses through social media, the daily deal sites came of age. In fact, it was in 2008 that Groupon became the second fastest online company to reach a billion-dollar valuation. It is estimated by Daily Deal Media (dailydealmedia. com) that by 2014, the worldwide opportunity for private sales and local deals together will be $40 billion.

Know Your Coupons, Daily Deals, and the Types of Websites

What's a Catalina Coupon you may ask? These are the coupons you find printed on your cash register receipt when you buy something at a store such as CVS, which often provides you with nearly an extra foot of coupons dragging from your receipt. Why Catalina? Because that was the name of the marketing company that came up with the idea.

Now that you know some trivia, let's see what kind of coupon and daily deal websites are out there. But first let's answer the $64,000 question.

What Is the Difference Between a Coupon and a Daily Deal?

- Coupons are typically for a small discount, and are presented for a savings on a product or service at the time of purchase. They are printed in newspapers or found online, printed, and then redeemed at the point of purchase. There is also the e-commerce online version of coupons, which come with a promo code that is then used when making an online purchase. This prevents the coupon from being used more than the number of times specified. Once the promo code is submitted the discount is subtracted from the purchase. The leading issuers of coupons are manufacturers, followed by retailers.

- Daily deals are prepaid deals, usually at a deep discount, in which you buy a product or service at a reduced price in advance. The buyer purchases a voucher for the product or service (more often services than products) and the transaction has been paid for. The voucher is then printed and given to the service provider. This, too, can be done electronically, utilizing the voucher number at the place of purchase. The leading issuers of daily deals are merchants.

Looking at the deals on restaurants, spas, and vacations on a daily deal site and the wealth of coupons for products offered by all sorts of manufacturers on a coupon site, you can immediately see a difference. At times, in this book, we will use the older

Coupon Sources

The most common type of coupon comes from manufacturers who offer a discount on their products at any participating location. By drawing people to new products in particular, many companies, such as Coca-Cola, have built up their consumer base. They continue to maintain customers by offering coupons on new products as well as on old favorites.

The other type of coupon is for a savings at a retailer, service provider, or another type of business. They provide a storewide discount on some of their products or services. This does not affect the wholesale price at which the retailer is buying an item, but is on the markup. Therefore, if they are purchasing an item at $5 and selling it for $10, they can offer a $1 coupon and their markup drops from $5 to $4.

"coupon" or "couponing" terms to cover the overall industry. Many of the general concepts, such as finding merchants and customers as well as building and maintaining a website, will apply to both online daily deal and online coupon businesses. In addition, many of the basic needs and principles of running a business—such as having a great business name and a web domain with excellent keywords for search engine optimization (SEO) purposes—will also apply to both online daily deal sites and online coupon sites.

The Three Types of Online Discount Websites

These are the three most common methods of offering discounts, with hybrids doing a little of everything.

Online Clipping Services

These are websites that provide coupons that you would otherwise clip from a newspaper, magazine, or a similar source (known as "clippers"). Examples include websites such as Coupons.com, CouponClippers.com, or RetailMeNot.com. These websites post numerous coupons from all sorts of manufacturers or merchants and make them available to consumers online. Shoppers go to the site, see what they want, and print out the coupons; they can then redeem them at their local stores. Note: When customers start printing coupons at home, they will first download quick and safe software from the site. Once installed, they can click away and get a ton of coupons. Remember, it's illegal to sell or photocopy coupons.

This online method simply makes it easier than going through the myriad of newspapers and literally clipping coupons. Most often, clipping sites sort coupons by the types of products offered. Typically, shoppers can also order coupons, but that is only feasible if it is a product they don't mind waiting for, since shipping the coupons takes time.

If you run such a coupon website, your sources of income include:

- A small percentage from the use of the coupons
- Serving as an affiliate to an established coupon website
- Selling advertising on your website
- Membership to your site
- A combination of these revenue streams

Daily Deal Websites

The hot trend, as evidenced by Groupon and LivingSocial as well as Eversave, Jasmere, and the eco-friendly Roozt, are daily deal sites, also known as group-buying sites. These offer deals that evolve through sales volume. In other words, the merchants offer large savings (often 50 percent or more) provided the website can produce enough volume to make it all worthwhile. Therefore, once the minimum volume is reached, which is typically very low, if there is one at all, the credit cards of customers who purchased the deal are charged and they can print out their vouchers, which are typically then redeemed at the store, restaurant, spa, resort, or wherever the merchant does business. Most of them are short-term, "daily deals" lasting one to five days. The objective is to grab people quickly and get impulse purchases before time runs out. This prompts the popular "buy now while supplies last" mentality. Mobile apps have made these deals even more accessible to consumers who can make a purchase while out and about, and swipe their iPhones or provide the code on their mobile device to the merchant.

These sites can be a boon to business for the merchants or, in some cases, a complete disaster. Business owners need to know how to turn one-time visitors and impulse buyers into long-term customers, or at least mathematically make the deal work for them. While that is essentially "their problem," it becomes your problem, too. If the merchants don't return with more deal features on your website, you also lose business. Therefore, one of your jobs will be to educate merchants on how to benefit from utilizing your coupon website—which is discussed later on.

If you run a daily deal website, your sources of income include:

- A cut, usually around 50 percent, of each deal
- Selling advertising on your website
- Membership to your site
- A combination of these revenue streams

While coupon sites use several of these means of making money, revenue for daily deal sites is primarily, if not exclusively, from taking a cut of the deals.

Coupon Referral and Aggregate Sites

These are sites that serve as a directory of sorts, pointing shoppers to where they can find deals, while helping various other coupon sites by offering a variety of their discounts all in one place. CoolSavings.com, for example, has everything from daily deals via LivingSocial and Groupon to coupons from manufacturers like Breyers, Betty Crocker, or Pillsbury. By affiliating with manufacturers, coupon sites, daily deal sites, and anyone else offering a coupon or discount, you become an aggregate or one-stop shop of sorts, with a database providing customers with many choices from which they can select the best deals. In an age of faster, faster, faster you are essentially narrowing down the field for consumers who can look at your site instead of ten coupon or daily deal sites. You can even offer side-by-side comparisons of products from different websites. The lazier we get as a society, the more such aggregate sites will continue to flourish, provided you offer a great variety of savings.

If you run an aggregate site, your main source of income will be a percentage from the various other sites with which you are working.

A Fourth Alternative

You could also be a deal site that does not offer "daily" deals, but instead features ongoing deals to members. Members pay a monthly fee and have access to savings on a regular basis from a wide range of merchants. The savings can change and new deals can be offered. However, members have access to many companies at all times.

Access Development has been doing this for years with affinity groups. For example, if you are a member of an auto club such as AAA, and the club offers membership discounts, it is likely working through Access Development or a similar type of membership deal service. You can also do this with individuals who join as members for a low monthly fee. In this case, it's kind of like having a membership at a shopping club such as BJs or Costco, only in this case your customers have access to more than 300,000 merchants from their computers or smartphones, by use of an app.

If you run a membership site, your main source of income will be from the monthly membership fees.

Finding Your Niche!

Regardless of the type of coupon or daily deal site you choose to run, it may be to your advantage to specialize, or find a niche. The increasing growth of the industry makes it harder for a new coupon or daily deal site to stand out. However, just as specialization has gained popularity in most other industries, the wave of the couponing and daily deal future will be to find a niche market. This will allow you to target your audience more closely and become known as "the place to go" for a certain genre of products and/or services. For example, if you become the premiere discount coupon site for school essentials, you can establish yourself in that area, offering students and their parents great deals on everything necessary for school. You might also offer schools special deals much the way other sites sign up affinity groups for special "group savings." For example, moms and dads will be able to find school supplies at a lower rate because they are parents of a student at Public School 126. From backpacks from several major manufacturers to graduation photo discounts, you could establish a niche as the back-to-school coupon or daily deal site.

> **Smart Tip** Tip...
>
> Consider how simply you can set up your website to be efficient and very user-friendly. Online coupon competition is fierce, so you can't afford to lose customers who are confused by your website. Make it easy to redeem coupons or deal vouchers.

Look for what you can offer that will entice people to become subscribers and regular visitors to your site. Is it an interest that your subscribers share? Is it a need that they all have in common? Is it an age range, such as teens or seniors? A lifestyle? Perhaps they are all residents of a town or community, and you provide the best deals in that area. If you find your niche early on, it will save you the trouble of trying to reach a massive audience when you can zero in on a more defined one and become the big fish in a smaller pond to start out.

Easy Market Research

If you're looking for a restaurant, it's likely that you'll ask for recommendations from friends and family. Likewise, if you're buying a new car, you probably have an idea of the cars your friends, family, and neighbors drive and whether you like the ride. You'll probably even test drive a couple of models if possible before making such a major purchase. Likewise, if you are opening your own business, you'll want to do plenty of market research.

First, let's assume that you are considering the possibility of launching an online coupon website because you are a fan of one or several such sites. It's likely that the impetus to start this particular business comes from some experience in the genre. Either you have had terrific experiences or you have come away frustrated and have the notion that you could possibly do better than the coupon sites you have visited. But don't take your own word for it.

Ask around. Ask your friends, family, and neighbors some simple questions, such as:

- Which coupon, daily deal, or deal websites do you use, if any?
- Are they easy to navigate?
- Do you need to become a member?
- Did they give you any gift or discount for becoming a member?

- How easy was it to redeem the coupons?
- Were there a lot of restrictions?
- Would you use that website again?

Typically, simple questions such as these will get people talking, especially if they landed a great deal or if they had a terrible experience. Remember, when someone has a good experience they tell 10 friends; when they have a bad experience they tell 30. Discounts, or lack thereof, are subjects people love to discuss. You should therefore come prepared. Let your "respondents" know that you are doing some informal research on the topic (coupon or daily deal websites) and record their answers electronically or with a pen and paper. Yes, taking notes by hand is still allowed. The point is, gather a lot of comments about these websites before even venturing into the arena.

Beware!
Some business owners think that a coupon or daily deal is some magical potion to end their sales lull—it isn't! While you can certainly share their optimism, don't get suckered into their pie-in-the-sky belief that this is the solution to all of your business problems. Before you order a new BMW, see how the coupons or daily deals work out for you first.

But don't just take everyone else's word for it—after all, they may have simply used the website incorrectly or just found a lucky deal. Join the sites, sign up, get their emails, and start browsing away. Go through the coupon or deal process on a number of sites and start getting a feel for the ones that you like and those that you do not care for. Take notes on what you like, what you don't like, and more importantly, what you could actually improve upon if you were to launch your own site. Also, read articles, blogs, and anything else you can find about the industry. You need to develop a competitive edge in business, and one way to do so is to learn about the competition from research, both first- and secondhand.

Merchants and Customers

For many business owners, making money comes from finding vendors and selling products to customers. In your case, you are not looking to purchase products to sell, but instead you want to serve as a go-between, or middle person, between the merchant or manufacturer and the customer. You are providing a service based on what the merchant/manufacturer is offering and the consumer is seeking. These are your most important relationships and both take time to establish and maintain.

Merchants: Quantity and Quality

The greater your selection, the more opportunity your potential buyers have to find something they want to purchase at a discount. However, quantity alone is not the solution. For example, offering daily deals at three Chinese Restaurants in the same town on the same day may not draw enough customers to any one of the three eateries to make it worthwhile for the owners. Hence, you may lose them all as merchants.

The quality of the products and/or services offered is also essential to making a go of a coupon business. Selling poor-quality products or giving travelers discounts to unsatisfactory hotels is not the kind of discount that is likely to attract repeat business to your website. Therefore, you will need to become discerning as a purveyor of quality offerings. Sure, it's hard to go wrong with coupons from major companies that have been around forever, BUT, that new restaurant down the street? Is it good? Subpar? How about the spa on the corner? Are they offering more than just massages? Quantity is nice, but quality offers are also important.

In short, you will need to know your merchants, who they are, what they offer, and if the Better Business Bureau has their name in bold letters and a sign that says "Beware" hanging in their office. Many people will be interested in offering savings, and these are your prospective clients. In most cases, you will be able to work out a deal that suits both of your needs. However, you need to know with whom you are forging a relationship since your reputation is on the line. You do not want to be aligned with businesses that do not come through on their deals, treat customers poorly, or are not legitimate.

Smart Tip

Tip...

Stay on top of what's going on. If you are posting coupons from major manufacturers (legally, of course), you can usually trust these major name companies. However, you will still need to stay alert, especially in a down economy. Major companies do go out of business and you do not want to get stuck with coupons or deals for companies that are folding, failing, or under investigation. Also see who is recalling products.

Your Customers: Discount Seekers

Who are these people?

Once upon a time it was your grand old aunt and your sweet grandmother sitting around the kitchen table in their not-so-fashionable bathrobes, cutting coupons from magazines. When you stood there questioning whether or not seven cents off on a can of corn was really worth all the trouble, you received the standard lecture on "a penny saved." Well, as one highly devoted, long-time coupon clipper explained, she saved as much as $15,000 in a year! So, perhaps it was worthwhile clipping those coupons.

The modern coupon clipper or savings seeker is likely to be anyone who uses the internet. Daily deals have become the thing to do, with many people emailing or texting their friends and family about their latest great find. Among the modern coupon seekers are:

Stat Fact

The coupon enthusiasts, most of whom are also quite computer savvy, know how to find whatever they are looking for. Jill Catalado, who runs a super couponing website, notes that research shows a disproportionate number of households in the $50,000 to $70,000 income range who fall into the "enthusiast" category of couponers.

- Moms and/or dads managing the household finances
- Anyone on a fixed income who has been hit hard by the economic doldrums
- Students
- The young upwardly mobile singles (or couples) who find a great deal "fashionable" and enjoy sharing it with their peers

Customer Statistics

There are also many wealthy customers seeking a good deal. A *USA Today* article from May of 2012 indicated that discount-coupon use among those who have household incomes of at least $100,000 is quite prevalent. Quoting a survey, they found that at least once per month, 71% use newspaper coupons, while 54% use online coupons. Nearly six out of ten 10 get digital "daily deals," with Groupon being the most popular service.

Is it a bigger trend among those who are not well educated? Nope. According to the same study, adults with college degrees were found to be almost twice as likely to have used coupons, in the six months previous to the study, as those who didn't graduate from high school.

The survey also found that "even if economic conditions improve, eight out of ten U.S. adults responded that they planned to continue to engage in couponing activities." This data was consistent then, and remains consistent now with other studies that show the popularity of digital (online, mobile) deals and coupons.

These are your potential customers—a broad base of individuals from various socio-economic classes, backgrounds, and education levels. As noted, they are your "potential" customers. You have to narrow down your niche, your target audience, and then go after them. They want deals, so they are out there and ready to listen, but you need to give them something that gets them excited.

Summary Points

- After more than 100 years of coupons in the United States, today's various types of coupon websites are doing very well. These include sites offering coupons that can be clipped for household necessities, such as groceries, to those offering daily deals for spas, vacations, or other luxuries.

- Online websites include those that offer the latest clippings for stores or manufacturer discounts, group-buying discount sites offering daily deals, and aggregate sites that post the best of a variety of deals from other leading sites for a small piece of the action. There are also membership sites that provide ongoing discounts to members. These are similar to shopping clubs.

- If this is the industry you have your sights set on, you should indulge yourself in some of the sites that are already going strong and do some grassroots research by asking friends, family, neighbors, and co-workers about their experiences with coupons and daily deals.

- Today's coupon clippers span a wide demographic range from students and individuals on fixed incomes to Yuppies, all looking to save some money and get a good bang for their buck. In fact, the wealthier sector is very much into couponing activities.

In the next chapter we'll turn inward so you can determine what it takes from you to not only get started in this business but to thrive. No business is right for everyone, so let's see if this is a good business fit for you.

Is This the Business for You?

Coupons? Deals? If you're thinking of going into this particular business, it's likely that you have a soft spot for discounts and savings. Whether you grew up in a household in which money was tight, learned the value of saving money from part-time or full-time jobs, or just love the thrill of finding a great deal, it is likely that you come to this industry with some passion for making wise choices when it comes to spending money. It always helps to do something for which you have a passion, especially when you will find yourself immersed in it as an entrepreneur.

But let's not get ahead of ourselves.

In this chapter, we'll look at:

- Starting a business—any business
- The pros and cons of starting your own business
- The necessary skills
- The lifestyle

Starting a Business, Any Business

Anyone deciding to go into his or her own business—whether opening a mom-and-pop shop, starting a part-time endeavor, buying a franchise, or starting a homebased, online business—needs to first think about what it means to be an entrepreneur.

Entrepreneurship is largely about the three P's: passion, planning, and perseverance. As mentioned above, anyone successful in business needs to have some passion for their choice of business. Restaurant owners love food, whether that means cooking it, being around it, eating it, or all of the above. The owner of a fitness center is typically someone in excellent shape, who values the hard work it takes to stay fit. And how often is the owner of a high-end dress shop wearing low-priced jeans? Not very often—typically a fashionable shop is run by someone with a passion for fashion.

Passion

If you feel passionate about good deals and are always looking to find methods of saving money and even forward such dollar-saving tips to friends and family members, you likely have what it takes to be in the coupon or daily deal business. Remember the old saying "Do what you love and love what you do."

Planning

Planning is paramount to starting any type of business. Most entrepreneurs spend numerous hours over the course of months or even years determining the many necessary details that will factor into their business. This includes everything from the business name to the business structure (sole proprietor, corporation, partnership, etc.) to attracting clients, attracting customers, designing a website, creating a marketing plan, and crunching numbers until you determine exactly how you will turn a profit.

You'll see, as you proceed through this book, how many factors go into running a business. Each takes careful planning, which explains why developing a business plan that outlines your business idea, your marketing strategy, and the business's financial goals can be extremely helpful. Whether you are seeking investors or using it as a means of guiding you through the process, a business plan is a great way of mapping out your business.

Perseverance

Perseverance is all about having the drive and wherewithal to keep on going through the many steps it takes to get started and run a business. It is about putting in long days, and sometimes, long nights to fine-tune your ideas and make sure they will work. For all of the businesses that launch every year, there are numerous others that die on the vine before even seeing the light of day. Often they fall short because the entrepreneurs did not have the unwavering determination to see them through to fruition. Perseverance also means being able to deal with and find solutions to the problems that will arise along the way. All businesses have problems. Whether it is getting the proper licensing, redoing a website that isn't quite right or isn't working as it should, or finding the right help, you will have your share of problems to overcome. You'll need to persevere, seek out answers, and keep on going.

So, do you have these three key attributes? Passion, planning, and perseverance are important to any type of business you choose to start.

The Pros and Cons of Starting Your Own Business

Before proceeding, it is wise to take a look at the big picture. Becoming an entrepreneur is very enticing to many people, especially if you are tired of always working for someone else, earning money

Bright Idea

Many small businesses are started as sidelines or part-time endeavors that grow slowly. In an unsteady economy, this is a cautious way to get a business off the ground. It means "keeping your day job" (hopefully one with a little flexibility) and sacrificing time spent elsewhere (typically in front of the TV). Thanks to the internet, you can start part-time and launch a small, part time coupon or daily deal business from the comfort of your own home. It's a way of getting your feet wet without diving in.

for other people, and/or dealing with office politics. Entrepreneurship allows you the flexibility you may desire and the opportunity to take control and reap the benefits and rewards of your own efforts. However, entrepreneurship is also fraught with great risk. According to the Small Business Administration (SBA), more than half of all new business does not survive the first year. So, here are the pros and cons to ponder as you think about starting a new business.

The Pros

- You have only yourself to answer to, meaning no more aggravation from the boss.
- You are the boss! You can create policies that you like, such as casual Mondays through Fridays.
- You can utilize skills that have been dormant in your career. Many passionate people with unused skills have flourishing companies because they were able to utilize talents and abilities they could not use in their 9-to-5 jobs.
- You have the flexibility to determine where and when you work. Many home-based business owners do much of their work at night.
- You have control over which direction your business takes and can shift gears quickly if you choose. This can be advantageous if economic or market conditions change and you want to adjust the products or services you offer—or even the look of your website. You do not have to go through "channels" and waste precious time waiting for nine vice presidents to sign off on a requisition to get a new wastepaper basket.
- The sky's the limit: Surveys have shown that four times as many millionaires evolve from their own businesses as those that work for someone else.
- You can choose your own team or you can fly solo for a while if you so choose. Many new business owners start out on their own or with a partner—but most of the successful ones know when to bring in key players who excel in areas that they do not. Since we all have our strengths and weaknesses, you can hire someone to do the bookkeeping if you hate crunching numbers, or to write your web copy if you simply hate writing.
- You can better arrange your work/personal life balance. Many entrepreneurs enjoy spending more time with their kids while they are growing up. Even if you are working in your office, you can always take some the time to spend with your family.
- You have greater control over your earnings since you can pay yourself first, as the saying goes. When the business is doing well, your wallet is getting fatter; when things are slow, you can determine where to economize. But you are not dependent on someone else to give you a paycheck, a raise, or a bonus.

- You can be as creative and out-of-the-box as you like—or not. It's your call.
- You have ownership, which means you can (if all goes well) sell the business someday if you wish. This is how many entrepreneurs make the big bucks.

The Cons

- You're the boss, which means if there's a problem, it's your problem.
- Launching a business means putting in a lot of hours. You'll hear people tell you that they put in 50, 60, or even 170 hours a week (which is two more hours than there are in a week) when they open a business. However, if you truly love what you are doing, some of those hours will fly by.
- Startup funding—you'll need to invest your own money and/or find others to invest in your ideas. This means having funding available that doesn't take away from the necessities of you and your family. For many new entrepreneurs, this also means maintaining an income from a spouse or significant other and having another job, meaning you may be putting in those 170 hours a week after all.
- There's a degree of risk as your liabilities increase. You'll need to protect yourself from those wanting to steal your ideas, steal your products, or sue you. From insurance to copyrights to trademarks to all sorts of online protection, you'll need to take charge of making sure you are safe from predators, including the viral ones.
- Nobody is paying you on a regular basis. There will be a stretch of time where you will not see any money. It typically takes at least one year, and very often two or three years, to show a profit. You need a financial cushion from somewhere.
- You have no backup, which mean no vacations for a while and working even when you're not 100 percent.
- You need to stay motivated even when you're ready to give up. This is a huge factor when it comes to failing businesses. Many people simply burn out trying to make a go of their own business.
- There are no guarantees, and even if you see some rewards, they may not last.

> **Tip...**
>
> **Smart Tip**
> Before starting a business, discuss your plans with an accountant, business advisor, and/or an attorney. Also research the licenses, permits, and taxes in your jurisdictions. You will need to have a business name and register your business with the IRS. Also make sure you cover any liability issues. Talk to your insurance agent.

▲

The Necessary Skills

According to Dave Bona, VP of Partnership Marketing at Access Development in the Greater Salt Lake City area, one of the most important skills in this business is being able to look at this industry from all sides. For nearly 28 years, Access Development has been building a network that now includes some 300,000 merchants offering discounts of up to 50 percent for organizations in virtually all U.S. markets. They are essentially in the deal-membership business offering deals to affinity groups. Bona, whose job is to bring merchants to Access Development, explains that you need to know how to look at the business from all perspectives before you can determine the best deal for the merchants and the customers. "You have to be on the other side of the counter with them to see how the business works from the merchant's side. Then, you have to show them what it looks like from the customer's side," explains Bona of the fine line between the merchant's offers and the customer's savings. "Each side needs to feel that they are getting something," adds Bona of what is essentially creating a win-win proposition.

Along with taking an overview of the business from both sides, Bona adds that you need to be flexible and creative because there are no real boilerplates. "Each business is different and you want to create the best deal for their particular needs and their market," adds Bona, who brought in 11,000 merchants in his first year with Access.

> ### Smart Tip
> *Tip...*
>
> Peruse coupon websites and see which designs you like. Some are more cluttered than others. Determine the look you want and count how many actual coupons are offered on a page on the sites you like. Study the ease of use and overall navigation. Take notes on the sites you find most user-friendly. This will give you an idea of what you want your website to look like.

The skill, Bona suggests, is the ability to look at all sides of a deal, and make it work for all parties involved, including you. Bona does acknowledge that he learned much of this on the fly during his first of what is now more than a dozen years in the business.

Marketing Skills

"If you build a website they will come." Well, that's clearly wrong. You need to make sure people know your website, and your business, exists. With that in mind, you need some marketing skills. Leveraging stale old ideas is the credo of the pseudo-marketing executives hanging onto their jobs with bright smiles and no original ideas. But it is not the way in which you start new a business and make it grow. No, you don't have to re-invent the wheel, but you do have to know how to put fresh ideas and new twists on what has worked successfully, and create your own market.

In this competitive business, marketing also means you'll need to build a subscriber base so that merchants have a reason to work their deals or run their coupons in your site. Marketing in this business means trying hard to build a subscriber base without spending too much money. "When it all started [the daily deal sites] advertising was cheap for [Google] AdWords and [Yahoo!] Keywords, but as the competition grew, so did the price of keywords and ad placement," explains Darrell Ellens, manager of the LinkedIn group Daily Deal Industry, and an expert and consultant in the industry. Ellens points out that when Groupon started, their cost of acquiring a new customer was $22; now it's gone up to $78.

What that means is that marketing-savvy entrepreneurs in this industry need to find ways to cost effectively draw customers, as well as merchants, to their websites. You can take some marketing courses and some social media classes to bolster your skills and get your creative juices flowing. You can also learn to utilize the many new tools that gather demographic information, such as sociographs (social graphs) and interest graphs in the internet context, which helps provide insight into what your target market is likely to purchase. More on marketing and using these graphs will be featured in Chapter 8.

Website Familiarity

No, you don't have to be a technical wiz; you can hire people to do the technical designing and building of your website. You can also hire people to work on updating it constantly if the task is not something in your area of expertise. But you do need to know what makes up a quality website and be able to express what you do and do not want to see on your site.

These, and additional keys to creating a great website, are discussed in more detail in Chapter 6, "You and Your Website." The point here is that you need to give significant attention to the numerous details that go into having a terrific website. Your business reaches the world through your website and your emails—make sure they are as good as possible. Remember to list the features you like and dislike from the many other coupon and deal websites that are already out there.

Attention to Detail

Attention to detail in this business means keeping accurate data on all of your merchants, their various deals, and all of your customers. Having a database is only part of the equation. You need to know how to access it and be diligent in maintaining your

12 Keys to Website Success

1. Excellent site design highlighting your deals and savings in a clear and inviting manner

2. Ease of use: you need to think of how quickly your customers can find coupons or deals and get them. In a competitive environment, you want the process to be seamless.

3. Simple deals (e.g., *10 percent off . . .; Save $1.25 on . . .*)

4. Clear and concise descriptions of the products and/or services

5. Ease of printing, online or electronic redemption

6. Ease of membership (Hint: Don't make them jump hurdles to join, or they won't.)

7. Offering enticements for returning (e.g., points programs, discounts for multiple purchases, etc.). You want your customers coming back to your site constantly.

8. Clear rules for customers and merchants

9. A posted privacy policy to which you adhere

10. Quality customer service that can be easily accessed

11. Good graphics—often graphics will save you many words

12. Clear visibility on mobile devices. Check this out because what you see on a laptop or desktop may not be the same as what others see on a smartphone

database. You will also need to keep tabs on numerous other details of running a business, including those pertaining to your employees (if you have any), bookkeeping and taxes (which you will have), plus business licenses, insurance, and more. Attention to detail is part of any business, but particularly one in which there may be many merchants, a large subscriber base and numerous specifics surrounding each coupon or deal you offer.

A Head for Numbers

Sure, you can hire someone to do your bookkeeping and your taxes, but this is very much a numbers game. Dave Bona, who's been in the coupon business for more than a decade now, says he can look at a restaurant menu and in 30 seconds know where they could offer discounts and not risk losing money. Of course, this comes with experience, but it also shows the importance of having a head for numbers.

Unlike a business in which you are buying a tangible product for $6 and selling it for $10, this is a business in which there are all kinds of deals using all kinds of numbers. You'll have coupons for 5, 6, 10, and 20 cents off, or deals for 50 or 60 percent off of a wide range of prices.

There are plenty of numbers involved in this type of business. For example, deals are all about savings, and that boils down to dollars and cents: **numbers.** Your cut of that deal is a percentage—again, **numbers.** Building your subscriber list, and at what cost? Again, **numbers.** You will need to be able to help your merchants determine how much of a discount they can provide and still make a profit—you guessed it, **numbers.** Yes, you are surrounded by numbers in this industry.

Sure, it's no problem posting a bunch of grocery store coupons such as the ones pictured on page 26, but, what do you get for doing so? Again, you need to determine the **numbers.**

Organizational Skills

Merchants on one side and customers on the other plus your web designer and your own bills to pay—there are a lot of elements that go into your single business entity.

Access Development has more than 300,000 merchants and numerous affinity groups, all with members taking part in the deals offered. They had better be well organized. Sure, it took them more than 25 years to reach that point and you are starting at a much smaller, manageable level. But if you don't have online and/or hard copy files, or both, plus backups of all of your data, you will be in trouble very quickly. The sheer number of components in this business calls for an excellent system of organization from day one. Otherwise you may get lost in a deluge of data.

While there are several software programs on the market, including coupon-specific ones such as CouponPaq.com, the age-old philosophy of *data in—data out* still holds true. Even in an age of "smart" technology, you are still the one responsible for entering the data and finding that data when you need it.

Merchant data needs to be constantly available and updated as they continue to create new deals for customers. You'll also need constantly updated customer data. Most of this can be done automatically. Merchants can even post and adjust their online deals as necessary. Obviously the customer experience should be handled through your technology. However, there are plenty of nuances and instances that will require you to step in. Having accurate data available and knowing which files to access can be crucial to maintaining your merchants and customers.

Sample of Manufacturer's Coupons

SAVE 40¢
on XYZ Soup

on any
THREE (3)
XYZ Soups

SAVE 55¢
on XYZ Greek Organic Yogurt

when you buy ONE 4-pack
of XYZ Greek Organic Yogurt

Prioritizing

Studies have shown that prioritizing (which goes hand in hand with good organization) is a key to success. Know your most important tasks and what can wait until later. Too many businesses have fallen on hard times because too much time was spent on incidentals and not enough on the most important areas such as paying bills on time and making sure to respond to the needs of clients (merchants) promptly.

In short, organizational skills are essential to doing well in this type of business.

People Skills

Are you a people person? As an entrepreneur in this type of business, you will be constantly using your people skills, at least while getting started. Unlike some online businesses where you can spend the vast amount of time quietly working on your computer, devoid of social contact, this job entails plenty of interaction.

While nobody says you need an outgoing bubbly personality, you do need some good professional interpersonal skills and the ability to open up clear lines of communication, especially with merchants who are putting a piece of their business in your hands.

You will typically be interacting with:

- Merchants
- Customer
- Your web team, such as designers and programmers
- Your staff, once your business grows

Listener Skills

The more diverse your offerings, the more you will need to tailor coupons to your merchants' needs. As Dave Bona pointed out, you will need to see how their business runs from both sides of the counter. In time, you will see similarities among like businesses, but you cannot assume that what worked for one bicycle rental business will work for another. You still need to listen to what the merchant wants and determine what you can provide.

You will also have your share of customer service needs. Again, much of your customer service concerns can be handled via technology, but as the business grows, so will the number of customers with questions, complaints, and concerns.

While coupons are pretty straightforward, you need to remember that you are in the service business, and as the middle person, you will need to be able to keep both sides happy. The key is listening and never assuming you know what the merchants or the customers are going to say.

Sales Skills

There are dozens of coupon sites. Why should a merchant post their deals with you? You will need to sell them on what you can offer and why it's better than the next guy. You will then need to sell your customers on why they should be looking for deals on your website. Sales skills are, therefore, important.

Since selling is more of an art than a science, you have a lot of room on your canvas to hone your own sales abilities. Selling is about establishing relationships, so you will need to determine the manner in which you can best forge such relationships. Not unlike impressing a date, this is based largely on your own personality. That being said, here are some sales basics that you will want to incorporate into your sales skills:

1. *Being a good listener*. This means you absorb what your clients, or merchants in this case, as well as your customers, are saying.

2. *Asking questions*. The best way to learn more about merchants or customers is to ask. While you don't want to fire questions at someone, you should not be afraid to ask pertinent questions.

3. *Knowing your products or service*. Not only must you be able to explain your business model and how your coupon or daily deal website works, but you need to do so with confidence.

4. *Having an edge*. This means being able to answer the question "Why should I go with your coupon site?" This is why you need to establish your competitive edge.

5. *Being respectful*. If you're condescending, you'll lose merchants and customers. If you are rude you'll also lose them. If you say or do things that are inappropriate—lose them.

6. *Knowing your merchants and/or consumers*. Due diligence is important prior to selling. Also know your target market. Be well versed in your prospective merchants and customers.

7. *Being clear and concise.* If a merchant tunes you out, you'll lose the sale. Don't confuse people; be direct. The best way to get from point A to point B is a straight line—likewise, be straightforward.

8. *Determining what needs of theirs you can fulfill.* Okay, so your merchants need more customers. How do you help them fulfill that need? Your clients want to save money. How do you help them meet that need?

9. *Working within their budget.* A good salesperson knows how to work from the mindset of their client. You'll want to look at the value of your coupons or daily deal from their perspectives. Make sure the deal is cost effective for your merchants.

10. *Building trust.* Sales is all about getting to know people and establishing a sense of trust.

So, Do You Have the Skills?

Stat Fact

It is estimated that over the past five years, roughly 600,000 new businesses were started annually in the United States. However, the SBA points out that fewer than half survived, or will survive, for five years. That's why you need to work hard at learning about your industry, your market, your merchants, and your customers.

If the skills mentioned above describe you, then you are a good candidate to launch an online coupon or daily deal website. If you have some of the above, you can start honing the other skills, and/or find other people who will help you. Remember, most businesses have more than one person involved at some level. While you may want to be on your own, it is to your benefit to find people who have the skills that you don't.

Review your skills and take stock of what you bring to the table. See "An Entrepreneurial Test" on page 30.

The Lifestyle

The entrepreneurial lifestyle is different than from of an employee. In this case, you will most likely be running the site from your home or a small office space to get started. You will need to motivate yourself, since there is no boss to motivate you, not even by threatening you. Money is always an issue for a new entrepreneur. Do you have enough to start the business, run the business, and cover the cost of living?

An Entrepreneurial Test

So, are you ready to be an entrepreneur? See what your answers are to the following:

- Are you ready to be "the boss" and take on all of the responsibilities that come with the title? _____

- Are you ready to make the sacrifices necessary to get a business off the ground? _____

- Are you ready to do your due diligence and research the industry and the business laws, etc., in your area? _____

- Are you prepared to stand behind a business 100 percent and sail onward to great success or go down with the ship? _____

- Are you ready to work really, really hard? _____

If the answers to the above questions are "yes," then you are ready to be an entrepreneur.

Unless you just inherited a fortune or have done very well in the stock market, as an entrepreneur, you will need to think about the costs of doing business and adopt a lifestyle in which you are watching your spending both in business and in your personal life, since your finances are typically tied closely together at first. Most new entrepreneurs are ready to make personal financial and time sacrifices to get their business up and running. For example, you will typically need to cut back on some aspects of your personal life, such as taking a long vacation or spending a lot of time at the movies or at nightclubs. Successful entrepreneurs will tell you that the sacrifices were well worth it. Those who tried and did not succeed often bemoan their lack of achievement but in many cases are glad they took a chance.

There is a learning curve to starting a business, meaning you'll need to learn about the industry, learn about your market, your potential merchants, your potential customers, and of course, your competition. You'll also need to learn the laws, rules, and ordinances involved in running your business, and these may vary by state, city, or county. Your lifestyle will, therefore, need to include allocating some time for educating yourself on all of the above. You may even take some courses or webinars on running a business, or on better sales techniques, or management or motivation.

Summary Points

- *Do you have the three Ps?* They are keys to your success. You want to have a *passion* for the business or industry, do a lot of advance *planning*, and have *persistence* to follow it all through.

- *There are a number of pros and cons to being an entrepreneur.* First is that you are the boss, which is both a pro and a con. It's a positive because you can make the decisions, alter your plans if you so choose, and do things your way. It is a negative because everything falls on your shoulders, you can't afford to take time off (while starting out), and when you make a decision you'll have to face the consequences for better or worse. You'll need to ponder all of the pros and cons before venturing forward. Essentially, the pros and cons come down largely to the glass half-full, glass half-empty theory. If the pros outweigh the cons in your eyes, then you are on the way toward being an entrepreneur. If the cons frighten the heck out of you, then you may not yet be ready to start your own business. Never fear, this can change with the economy, your life situation, your financial situation, and your desire to take a chance. Many people today are business owners who never before envisioned themselves in such positions.

- *There are several skills in particular that will help you excel at this type of business.* They include: marketing skills, familiarity with having a business website, attention to detail, organizational skills, people skills, listening skills, a head for numbers, and sales skills.

- *The lifestyle of an entrepreneur differs from that of an employee working for someone else.* You need to be at the ready 24/7 for whatever can go wrong. You will likely need to make some sacrifices in order to devote the time and money necessary to start and run a business. You will have to do your homework and be ready to work hard. It can pay off handsomely, but there are no guarantees.

In the next chapter we will go into more how coupon and daily deal businesses operate.

How It Works

We've given you a brief industry overview and a little history. We've defined the different types of coupon and daily deal sites out there and also talked about the skills necessary to handle such a business. Now, let's talk shop.

How do you get a coupon or daily deal site off the ground?

There are four key elements of either type of online business—whether coupons or daily deals:

1. Your network of customers
2. Your website
3. Your merchants
4. Your marketing

Ironically, as easy as it would seem to work in this progressive order, building a site, getting merchants to feed you coupons or daily deals, and then marketing such great discounts to an audience, it's not quite as easy as it sounds. Sure, if this were a brand-new idea, merchants would be interested in drawing customers and might very well take a chance that you can market your new idea to millions of people. Today, however, the chicken and egg story becomes part of the equation. Why should a merchant sign up for your site if you have no followers, no audience, no potential customers? And why should customers sign up if you have no merchants?

There is one other important factor to be considered even before examining the ways in which you will proceed with all of the above, and that is your revenue stream. How will you make money? With all of that in mind, let's proceed through this chapter as follows:

- Making money
- Building (or having) a following
- Your website
- Your app
- Your merchants
- Getting coupons
- Coupon affiliates
- Aggregator sites

We'll leave marketing for its own chapter!

Making Money

There are a few ways in which your coupon or daily deal website can make money. They include:

- *Commissions from sales.* This is the primary manner in which daily deal sites make money, typically as much as 50 percent of the deal price. Coupon sites also get a piece of the action as well. The "click here" for a coupon transmits the coupon site information to the vendor. You then get commissions from the vendors, which in this case may be the manufacturers. You can also be set up to send the visitor directly to the merchant's site when he or she clicks on a coupon of interest. Then, if a sale is made, you get a commission from the merchant.

- *Sales.* No, you cannot sell coupons. But if you choose to sell a book on extreme coupons or something that suits your specific niche, you can sell your own products or services. If, for example, you are posting coupons or daily deals in a geographic region, you can sell guidebooks to that region or other regional goods.

- *Membership.* Daily deal sites and coupon sites have largely abandoned membership since they make money from a portion of sales on the merchant's end. However, if you want to be a deal membership site, group, or club, you can make your revenue by charging a monthly membership allowing your members access to ongoing deals from many merchants.

- *Advertising.* Banner ads are one way to make money. You will need to have a lot of traffic to sell such advertising. If you have a niche, reach out to businesses in the same area of interest.

- *Data.* Some aggregator sites make money by gathering and selling marketing and analytical data to the various daily deal websites with which they are working.

- *Affiliate programs.* Many coupon sites offer affiliate programs. They offer bonuses to each person for referring new people to the site and/or a cut of whatever business comes through your referral sites from the referral code. This is a great way to start out and make some money. Many sites, such as Coupons.com, have affiliate programs. In essence, you bring them customers and business, and they pay you for doing so. You'll find more on coupon affiliate programs later in this chapter.

- *Blog.* Sharing coupon information in a blog can lead to money from affiliates. It's important to build a professional-looking blog and have plenty of good content, which can include coupons, special offers, sidebar advertisements, etc., on your site, and earn money

> **Tip...**
>
> **Smart Tip**
>
> Starting out as an aggregate website can be a great way in which to generate commissions without having to find the merchants yourself. Instead you can look for affiliate programs offered by other sites. For example, CoolSavings.com features grocery coupons and has an affiliate program whereby your site can link to theirs and you can benefit from their sales. Your job will be to draw visitors to your site.

when someone follows the link to a product and makes a purchase. The difference here is that you are not simply posting coupons but providing content and updating it to bring your audience back often. Visit some coupon blogs to get an idea of what yours can look like. Popular ones include; CouponQueen. com, BargainBrianna.com, DealSeekingMom.com, and Hip2Save.com Among the many affiliate networks you can join when you start a website and a blog are ShareASale.com, Commission Junction (cj.com), Coupons.com, CoolSavings. com, and LinkShare.com.

Building (or Having) a Following

Okay, this does fall in the realm of marketing, since you are building a customer base. But here you are building a subscriber list to get started.

LivingSocial boasts more than 30 million subscribers, while another popular coupon site boasts more than 800,000 followers on Facebook alone. Do not despair: You can run a coupon or daily deal site successfully and earn money with a much smaller subscriber base. Nonetheless, building a following is what business today is all about (not just in this industry).

Your first goal when looking to build a following—hence a subscriber list—is to determine who makes up your target market. While it is hard to compete head to head with Groupon, LivingSocial, or Coupons.com, one of the most fertile areas of potential growth in the coupon or daily deal industry is being part of the niche market. There are two ways to approach finding a niche market. One is to utilize your current environment and build from that base. For example, if you are attending or working for a college and have a means of reaching 20,000 students to ask them to subscribe to your new discount site, then your niche should be in line with what students at your university really want. A well-known chef, for example, might tap into his foodie following and culinary connections with a deal site featuring anything food related.

Alternatively, if you do not have such a potential following on hand, you will need to use your knowledge in a particular area of interest and do your homework. Are you going to build a site centering on sports-related deals? Coupons for fashion and clothing? Travel items only? Become THE place to go for products and/or services in your niche area and you can corner the market. Add blogs on the topic, interviews with notable people in the field, ads from related businesses, and even endorsements from celebrities, and you can have a very successful niche website. Sites such as CellarThief. com for wine lovers, BarkingDeals.com for pet owners, and Jetsetter.com are examples of successful niche deal sites.

In the end, it is imperative that you start thinking about how you will build your following from day one. Your goal is to have a list to which you can email your daily deals, latest coupons, and /or newsletter. It is also to draw people to your website for more offers.

Some daily deal sites emerge from individuals who already have a large following. They have been started by radio station managers, newspaper publishers, and others who already have a large subscriber base. You may be able to partner with someone who fits the bill by using their list and your hard work to get the business off the ground. Make sure their list is a subscriber list and not just a purchased list or something put together illegally. You can share commissions and get started more quickly if you use such a strategy. Of course you will also have to have a similar vision for the business and be a good match or you may be asking for more trouble than their subscriber list is worth.

If you have such a base, you're ahead of the curve; if not, you can build it (by putting in the hours), and they will come.

Niche Ideas

There is always the simple niche of a local coupon site, not unlike the coupon books that for years were handed out door to door or arrived in the mail. Only now, you can expand from local merchants to online businesses, which can be based anywhere with special deals for your ZIP code (or ZIP codes) in your regional area. Darrell Ellens points out a gentleman in Vancouver, who analyzed his niche market very carefully and found local deals for them. He has only about 3,000 to 4,000 subscribers, but from that he has an astonishing 30-percent buy rate. "The guy has all of the people and merchants in a couple of postal codes, so he has a very hyper group of local subscribers," adds Ellens, who runs the Daily Deal Merchants group on LinkedIn (as well as the Daily Deal Industry group).

WhereYouShop.com also takes a localized approach, providing members upon signing up with a local map where they can pinpoint places frequently visited. Offers are then emailed to members based on these predefined areas only, so that their inboxes are not flooded with offers outside of their area and interests.

Another popular site, simply called DailyDeals.com, decided not to go local at all and only provides deals to "online only" stores. The hope is to attract online businesses and build a following through email and Facebook.

You can also select one segment of the market, whether it's the millennial generation of young people born between 1982 and 2002 or the ever-popular baby boomer generation nearing retirement. You might want to research the buying trends of this target group.

Subscriber Base Building

Technology today can help you localize and/or specialize by targeting a demographic area or group. Of course, you can't get anyone to your website until it is built. But planning how you will build your following is imperative to your success. Some of your sources will include:

Social Media

As you build your site, plan your Facebook fan page, and look for as many people to "Like" you as possible, invite everyone you can think of and ask everyone to invite their friends. Grow your following!

Start tweeting on Twitter and again, build a following. Also, attract attention. For example, you might hold a contest, take a poll, make a Twitter-only free offer, ask a question, or start a hashtagged discussion thread (a keyword that begins with the # sign).

Use LinkedIn to talk about your new deal or coupon site in groups and build your number of connections. Don't blatantly promote yourself, but enter discussions and let it be known that you are looking for people who want to save money.

Use your Twitter, Facebook, or other social media websites to offer friends and followers a special discount. Make the promotions compelling so that your followers feel special. After all, they're following you for a reason: To get great deals! You can also create Facebook and Twitter accounts that will broadcast online deals with status updates that direct viewers back to your website.

Start a blog on your website with links to your posts all over the social media to draw people to your site.

The Brick-and-Mortar World

Don't ignore real people in real places. Promote yourself in all local businesses that will let you, especially your merchants. You can offer to hold a contest in a store and give something away. Have people put their business cards in a bowl and collect it at the end of the week—those are all people that are now on your email list. Have fliers, posters, and other means of drawing people to your site

> **Bright Idea**
>
> Be omnipresent. Yes, you'll have to sleep sometimes, but simply posting on Facebook, tweeting on Twitter, and linking in on LinkedIn is not enough. Once your site is built, you'll need to put in the hours online to build and maintain those connections. And if 24/7 is a little much for you, find friends, relatives, or hire someone to help. The point is that you want to answer questions and make yourself available to anyone, anytime they need it, reassuring your followers and letting it be known that you are enthusiastic about what you have to offer.

as well as sign-up sheets where people can put their email addresses to receive a newsletter about saving money. Then do a short online newsletter with money-saving tips.

Smart Tip

Once you have a niche (and a website), use that niche to start making social media connections with like-minded people who are more likely to have an interest in what you have to offer.

Get Yourself Listed

Local or niche-centered directories are numerous, both nationally and locally. Find out what you need to do to become listed.

Get on YouTube

Make a short video about your niche area of interest. Make it entertaining and "unusual" within the bounds of reasonably good taste so that it can go viral. And remember to let them know about your great discounts!

Make Them Come Back for More

Once you get people to your site, offer them rewards, discounts, bonus points (toward something free), or additional savings if they come back for more. Also, providing regular content can help you bring them back.

Use Star Power

No, it's not easy to find someone with a name to join forces with you, but if you know a celebrity, see if you can get an endorsement. A sports discount or coupon site needs an athlete; a food and restaurant site might benefit from a known chef; and a local site might utilize the services of a local celebrity. The point is, they can plug their latest book, speaking engagement, or anything else if they can also help you build your list from their following. Celebrities don't come cheap, so if you can't work out a satisfactory deal, or if you don't simply know someone, this may be a costly means of growing your business. Several deal sites are affiliated with celebrities.

Advertise

Use the power of Google AdWords, Yahoo! Keywords, or other online advertising to get the word out—just know your keywords in advance and watch your expenses closely.

Public Speaking

You're now a new expert on saving money. Use that, or any other area of expertise, to speak at the local libraries, meetings of groups or associations, community centers, or any place else that has public speaking. Have a sign-in sheet for names and email addresses.

3 / How It Works

▲

Celebrity APP

The new Yowza!! Mobile Coupon app got a huge boost because co-founder Greg Grunberg starred in the NBC series *Heroes.* Grunberg not only had a large following but had celebrity friends available for helping with promotions. Likewise, endorsements by Bobby Flay are drawing customers to the new shopping site Open Sky. If you know someone with a large following, see if they want to lend their name. Play on their celebrity status—celebrities typically have big egos.

Your Website

Once you have your domain name (see Chapter 4, "Boring Business Basics"), you'll be ready to build your website. You can do this yourself (typically through an online template), hire a web designer, or get a web design company to do it for you. Your choice will depend upon your technical abilities and your flair for design.

If you're anxious to get a site up and working for your daily deal business, you can opt to use a software program like Daily Deal Builder (www.dailydealbuilder.com), a 100 percent ready-made group deal site for your business from the HC Consulting Group. Having such a daily deal platform makes it easy to populate the fields with your own deals. "We offer flexible options to give our clients the ability to have full code access to do anything they want or hire out our team if they choose," says Marc Horne, co-creator of Daily Deal Builder, who also recommends that daily deal site owners do something to stand apart and not just be another cookie-cutter site. When it comes to running the site, Horne points out that 95 percent of the users utilize an admin panel designed to take the technical know-how out of the equation and leave busy entrepreneurs with more time to run their daily deal businesses. "The admin panel lets you input the title of the deal, the sale price, choose the dates that it will run, the graphics, and so on. Then it automatically puts up the start time and pulls the deal down at the end time," explains Horne of the new technology, which can be customized to meet the need of the site owner. While Daily Deal Builder is not a business model, it is a platform on which you can run your daily deal business.

Another daily deal platform comes from Deal Current (www.dealcurrent.com), which also provides a full-service daily deal site without the fuss and muss of building

Stat Fact

According to sales researchers, coupon sites and daily deal sites are listed as among the top five reasons why people buy smartphones.

one from scratch. Deal Current also offers unlimited design and styling with the site owner (you) in control.

These two major players in the daily deal site industry run roughly 500 daily deal sites. There are several other major companies in the field, such as NimbleCommerce (www.nimblecommerce.com). If you search for daily deal building platforms or software, you will find various choices.

If you're starting a coupon site, there are also platforms to make your life easier such as CouponPress (couponpress.com), which works along with WordPress (a website building tool) to provide you with all the necessary tools for creating coupons, updating and managing your website, and even indexing your coupons in search engines through SEO technology. There are plenty of other coupon software programs out there, such as Coupon Fusion (www.couponfusion.com) or Coupon Script (www.couponscript.org) that provide all the necessary ingredients for creating and uploading coupons onto your website. These programs are designed for easy use and flexibility, and come with customer support should you have any questions.

The bottom line is that you can hire a web designer and have them build a site, but the backend needs of a daily deal or coupon site will require someone with some tech experience in the field, and that can be costly. The platforms and software programs available today make good sense unless you, or someone you know, are savvy at site building or unless you have a big budget to hire a web design company to build such a site from scratch.

Priorities

While we talk more about the look and feel of your site later on, your priorities on a daily deal or coupon website include:

1. Easy to create deals or coupons
2. Ease of printing or online redemption
3. Automatic posting and removal of offers
4. Quality graphics
5. Backup and data storage (you want to save old coupons for future use)
6. Simple customer service capabilities

Number six means that you, or someone designated by you, will need to provide customer service. You'll also need to work on your search engine optimization (SEO),

Stat Fact

America is not alone when it comes to the daily deal phenomenon. Countries all over the world are rich in such sites. In Europe, for example, you'll find the United Kingdom has 82 such sites, followed by: France, 76; Greece, 75; Netherlands, 66; Poland, 65; Bulgaria, 56; Germany, 43; Spain, 39; Italy, 37; and Croatia has 35. While these numbers will change, the point is deal sites are global.

which is crucial today if you want customers to find you among the numerous coupon and daily deal sites out there. While platforms and software will help you in this area, only you can determine which keywords will set you apart from the masses.

We'll talk more about the look and feel of your site, as well as finding a hosting service, in Chapter 6, "You and Your Website."

Your APP-lication

To compete today, you will want to look into the mobile world of applications, or *apps*, as they are better known. From daily deals to coupons to membership discount sites, apps are allowing customers to find the nearest deal and benefit from saving money wherever they are and whenever they choose. From a gym to a diner to a spa to the Gap, consumers can find all sorts of opportunities in any location. "Yowza!! delivers digital coupons directly to shoppers' smartphones while they are actually shopping in the store," says David Teichner, CEO of Yowza!!, which was one of the first apps launched in the daily deal industry.

While Yowza!! may have beaten you to the punch, you can also offer an app to expand your horizons. Clearly, with more than 200,000 apps already available, it can't be that difficult. But, not unlike your website, you'll need the data before the app can be worthwhile.

Also, not unlike building a website, you can use online services to build your app, such as those at Mobile Roadie (www.mobileroadie.com) and The App Builder (www. theappbuilder.com). From app-building platforms you will also be able to get your app onto iPhones, Androids, and so forth. You can also look into a browser-based platform such as AppMakr to make an iPhone app, or GENWI, which lets you create and manage your app on a variety of mobile devices, including your iPhone, Android, and HTML5.

Of course, you can build an app on your own if you are somewhat tech savvy and can follow instructions. Apple provides app-building instructions, and if the length of the website address doesn't scare you away, it might be something you can consider. Apple's instructions for apps are at: https://developer.apple.com/library/ios/#documentation/UserExperience/Conceptual/MobileHIG/Introduction/Introduction.html.

There are also books and other websites (Google "how to create an app") on how to build an app.

The other alternative is to hire an app developer. Once again, you'll find plenty of companies and individuals who build apps on the internet. There is probably even an app for finding app developers. Prior to hiring an app developer, read up on the various features that can be included in an app. The basic criteria for you to consider are:

- Cost
- Time
- Experience (especially with this type of app)
- Ability to meet your data needs (understands what you want)

After locating several potential developers, meet with them to determine how they work, how much they charge, and if they can provide references. You will likely hear prices in the $2,000 to $10,000 range. Get a few quotes before making a decision. The cheapest isn't always the best if someone else has more experience in this type of app. Keep in mind the price will depend on the level of complexity and how much work, if any, you've already done. You can read up on how to do a layout and an app design, just as you would lay out your website. Doing this in advance and having a clear idea (from looking at other apps) of how you'd like to see your app work can reduce the price.

BUT, get your website done first! You'll need data for the app to access; it does not come loaded with merchants for you.

Your Merchants

Daily deal sites need deals and coupon sites need coupons. While there are several ways in which you can procure coupons, daily deals will come primarily through building relationships with merchants or having sales reps do that for you.

It's imperative that you know what you can offer the merchant in a competitive field. First, you will have to build up a subscriber base. As mentioned earlier, building a subscriber base is time consuming, but not particularly difficult because people want good deals. The only drawback in the beginning is getting people to sign up when you have no deals to offer. Therefore, you will have to let people know what is coming and provide content about deals and savings and all sorts of good things on the topic.

With a little good salesmanship, you can get those first merchants on board. In most cases, they have nothing to lose.

Merchants need to know that you understand their needs and their parameters, such as how many customers they could possibly serve. For example, a 100-seat restaurant cannot manage 500 people redeeming a voucher in one night. As Dave Bona, who manages merchant acquisition for Access Development, mentioned earlier, "Each side needs to feel that they are getting something." After all, you want a deal that works so that your merchants return as well as your customers.

Know What You Want

The task of finding merchants comes down to first knowing what you are looking for. What is your demographic area and what type of merchants fit the bill? You'll want to find and connect with merchants who target the same buyers as your site. Therefore, if your site is geared toward the foodies, go after restaurants, gourmet shops, and specialty food stores. Are you selling sports-related deals? Look for sporting goods shops, stores selling outdoor apparel or camping equipment, campgrounds, skating rinks, or venues that hold sporting events. Are you all about parenting? How about clothing or toy stores for kids, indoor play spaces, family friendly eateries, children's museums, or bookstores that have a wide selection of children's books? Narrow your field to your target audience and prepare to tell them what is special about your site. Keep in mind that the larger players cannot provide the personal attention that you can. As the industry grows, the smaller deal sites that offer greater attention to merchants will become important players.

Getting Your House in Order

Looking for merchants means having your website and/or app ready to roll, having some level of a subscriber base, and knowing what kind of deals you are offering. Groupon deals must be at least a 50-percent discount and are then a 50-50 split between them and the merchants on each sale. However, merchants who have run Groupon deals before have reported that their sales reps are open to working favorable splits that benefit both parties. You have to know ahead of time what type of deal will and will not work for your business.

You'll also need to determine the time frame. Some sites offer one-day deals only. Others have deals that are featured for one day but are then moved back on the website for a couple more days.

What is the tipping point at which the deal kicks in? The "tipping point" is the term used to describe the minimum number of buyers at which the deal will go into effect. This is to protect the business against loss. For example, if the value is on a three-hour cruise and there is a cost to running it, the merchant might need a certain amount of passengers to make it worthwhile. If they are running a deal on your site and they don't reach their minimum, the deal gets canceled and customers do not lose their money, nor does the cruise lose money by sailing with only three people. However, many daily deal sites, and their merchants, no longer bother with a tipping point. If you use one, make it something low such as 10 percent of the available units. You need to address this with the merchants.

Refund policies also need to be worked out. One long-term deal site basically says don't bother them if the deal is no good—so it's buyer beware. The problem is that there is a lot more competition today, meaning that customers may not like such a policy. Merchants may not like the lack of support, either.

Most significantly, you'll need to have a contract that merchants will sign explaining what both of you are offering. You are serving as the go-between for merchants to promote a deal for x number of days through your website and emails (and a newsletter if you have one). You will send it out to x number of people in a specific geographic region. Remember, deals for a restaurant in Cleveland do not attract buyers in Boca Raton. So, if you are selling merchants on the visibility they will get, it has to be realistic, otherwise you are misleading them and will get a bad reputation. Note: Other than online businesses, most daily deals are for local merchants—so make sure you are serving their area. You need to set a minimum

What Do Merchants Want from You?

It's important to have an idea what merchants are looking for from daily deal sites. The general consensus shows that merchants focus on:

1. Your reach—how many subscribers you have or will have

2. A reasonable, and even flexible deal structure

3. Your website—Does it look professional and is it available 24/7?

4. Customer service—Can they reach you if there is a problem?

5. Easy payment terms—Make it clear how and when they will get paid.

6. Options for mobile customers

discount that they must provide (Groupon's is 50 percent), and then you need to set your commission, which in many cases starts at 50 percent.

You also need to detail how they will get paid. Will you send all of the money three weeks after the deal ends? Will you send it in two or three payment? How long will people have to wait to receive their money? Hint: They don't like to wait very long, so try to create a short turnaround time.

Finally, add in all eligibility requirements, such as only one deal per customer, age requirements, such as no one under 21 for a wine tasting, and so on. In the end, have an attorney look over your standard agreement.

Seeking Merchants

Once you have everything in place, especially a contract, you can start seeking merchants. Looking for merchants means going to business directories, depending on your geographic and demographic needs. It can mean contacting the local chamber of commerce, major retail or restaurant chains, or specific businesses with your offers. Localeze (localeze.com) is a great resource for finding businesses in your area. Superpages™ is a national Yellow Pages directory that can also help you make lists of prospective merchants. It's not hard to make up a business list in your area or region. Businesses are all around you, so start zeroing in on the ones you want to approach. Be careful to be neither too narrow in your focus, nor too broad. You want a lot of merchants but you also want those that fit your niche.

There are also industry lists available depending on your niche. You can buy such a list or strike up a partnership with a company that has lists of merchants. If you Google "mailing list," you will find numerous companies that sell them. However, if you can find someone who has used a mailing list, find out where they purchased it and if it was up-to-date and worthwhile.

The Savvi Story

How would like to start your website off with 300,000 merchants? Yes that's 300,000! After two years in the building stage, Savvi (www.savvi.com) launched in the spring of 2012, offering both a website and an app to create a membership deal site. Using the Costco, Netflix, and Hulu business model of offering consumers one low monthly fee for membership, Savvi opted for an ongoing unlimited deals model rather than daily deals.

Good plan, but how did they get so many merchants, you ask? Very simple. "I met with the CEO of Access Development, a company that has been running deals for affinity groups for over 30 years," says Darin Gislon, CEO of Savvi. "During that time they had built a massive network of merchant relationships and now have over 300,000 merchant locations in their network," explains Gislon, who offered a new value proposition to Access Development. Noting the rapid rise in mobile technology, Gislon and his team offered to provide an app that could utilize this massive merchant database for individual consumers on a membership basis. Up to now, Access Development was highly successful offering deals to affinity groups, as mentioned earlier. They had not yet tapped into the individual market, nor did they have an app of their own.

The end result was that Savvi launched a website and an app with Access Development's 300,000 merchants for individual members.

So, why are we telling you this? Savvi, like other established sites, offers an affiliate program to people like you. What this means is that from the Savvi website (www.savvi.com), you can become an affiliate and offer your customers 300,000 merchants. Yes, that's 300,000 merchants! Savvi will provide you with a landing page, which you can customize and link from your site. What is particularly attractive about this type of affiliate deal is that unlike other affiliates which typically offer you a percentage only on each sale, you get a percentage each month of the membership fee for each member you get to sign up. Therefore, if you bring in 1,000 members who join Savvi from your site, you'll have a few thousand dollars a month to add to your income.

Getting Coupons

There are several ways to get coupons for your site, none of which is buying them. Coupon sales are illegal. The first means of getting coupons is to work out deals with merchants and have them send you coupons on a regular basis. An established business will be able to send you their coupons to post on your site.

Smaller businesses may not have such a program set up, so you will need to work out deals. Larger companies, however, often have coupon affiliate programs, and you need only to demonstrate why they should add you as an affiliate. This means having that large subscriber base as mentioned earlier and/or a great niche. You can then have an XML (Extensible Markup Language) feed set up, which means a computer-to-computer delivery of coupons or coupon codes to your site on a regular basis. If you are working with coupon newbies, you will need to design coupons for them. You can use a software program for creating coupons such as Couponpaq (www.couponpaq.com) or opt for an online service such as Coupon Fusion (www.couponfusion.com) for just $9.95 per month. They offer coupon designer software, online clipart, and the always important technical support.

Looking at other coupons will give you an idea of how to design your own coupons featuring the product or store and the savings in bold, clear print, with a graphic to illustrate, but not detract from, the deal. Remember, people browse coupon pages quickly, so a deal needs to jump out at them. Also remember to include all of the important stipulations from the expiration date to the limit per customer to the "while supplies last."

Examples:

Valid through 12/12/11—one coupon per customer per service offered. Valid with coupon only / Not valid with any other offer.

Valid through 12/12/11 only while supplies last. Limit 1 per customer

Look at the fine print on other legitimate coupons for the fine print so you can phrase yours accordingly—and clearly!

In an age of social media, people are sending coupons to each other all the time, so why not share them with a website such as yours? This is how many sites, such as DealsForMommy.com and the extremely successful RetailMeNot.com, get many of their coupons.

There are, however, two inherent problems with getting coupons from wherever you can find them. First is you're not going to make any money. If you establish a relationship with a merchant, you also establish a means of making money from them through the coupon code. If, however, you have people sending you coupons, you'll need to have advertising, membership, or another source of revenue.

The second problem is getting reputable coupons. This means coupons that are viable and actually usable from the stores or manufacturers. The bottom line is that you are taking a major risk getting coupons from anywhere. They may be fraudulent, dated, stolen, copied, or obtained in some illegal manner—plus you may jeopardize your computer (with a virus) and your business's reputation.

Unfortunately, the internet has become a haven for fraudulent coupons. In fact, CouponIntegrity.com, a website trying to help maintain ethics in the industry, lists several codes of coupon ethics for consumers, which include using coupon

> **Beware!**
> While affiliate programs are a great way to get started in a very competitive industry, don't be discouraged if they do not come easily. They can take some time. You'll need patience and persistence. Many successful coupon and daily deal sites are the result of at least two years of slow building. You need to continually work on the chicken and egg problem of getting both merchants and subscribers little by little.

sites that promote obtaining coupons in only ethical manners and not from third-party clipping services. They point out that coupons should be approved by the manufacturer. Obviously the easiest way to make sure of this is to deal directly with the manufacturers yourself or with affiliate programs that have a reputation of dealing with the merchants or manufacturers.

On your website and/or app, you want to feature coupons that:

- Meet the manufacturer's or merchant's parameters, meaning they adhere to the limits per family or customer
- Have coupon codes that work
- Are not already expired

In short, you must be vigilant when getting coupons to make sure they are of value to the users and obtained legally.

Coupon Scams

Depending where you look, you can find some big bucks posted as rewards for bringing coupon scammers to justice. Yes, thanks to the ease of making coupons and posting them on the internet, the proliferation of fraudulent coupons is growing rapidly. The Coupon Information Corporation (CIC), a nonprofit association of consumer product manufacturers dedicated to fighting coupon fraud, estimates that coupon scams cost $300 to $600 million a year. The CIC has helped authorities crack numerous coupon scams leading to the arrests of the perpetrators.

One of the most obvious of the illegal practices, when it comes to coupons, is selling them or auctioning them off, which is illegal but doesn't stop many websites from doing so. More difficult to catch are the fake coupons that look like the company (or store) originals, but are not. This is why you need to work with reputable sources.

Some tips that you may be looking at a fake coupon include:

- Free products—most coupons are not for something free
- Spelling and grammatical errors—most stores know how to spell their own business name and before offering a coupon, they typically proofread the fine print
- No expiration date—almost all legitimate coupons have an expiration date
- Unfamiliar logo—an altered or unfamiliar logo may be someone's attempt to duplicate the coupon of a store or manufacturer. Look at the company's website and compare the logo and any graphics with those that you think are altered or bad duplicates.

- Bogus amount—most coupons are for a small amount off of the price. A coupon for $5 off of a $9 item may be quite bogus. Note that the daily deal sites do have savings of 50 percent or more. But those are on larger items sold to x number of people. Coupons are not the same type of deal so do not expect such savings from a legitimate coupon.

As emphasized earlier, the source of the coupon is also in question, which means using coupons from anyone anywhere can be troublesome until you learn to recognize bogus coupons. If you want to check out some of the ones being circulated you can go to the CIC website at http://www.couponinformationcenter.com.

The folks at MoneySavingsQueen.com remind you to "stick to manufacturer websites and well-known websites such as Coupons.com, RedPlum.com, and SmartSource.com."

Coupon Affiliates

There are good affiliates and bad affiliates, depending on how they obtain coupons and whether or not they pay you as they say they will. You need to work only with affiliates using approved manufacturer or store coupons. You can apply to work with an established coupon site or a merchant or manufacturer that has an affiliate coupon program. What happens when you use an affiliate program is that your website displays the coupon with a voucher code. When a visitor clicks on the link it may go to the merchant's site or to a landing page on your site provided by the affiliate company, the merchant, or the manufacturer. Then, if the visitor makes a purchase, the merchant knows that the visit was through an affiliate link. So the affiliate—that's you—is credited with a commission (the affiliate's share of the sale), and this is the income from the site.

Coupon Feed (couponfeed.net), for example, offers a legitimate affiliate program that includes coupons from thousands of merchant feeds and network feeds as well as from affiliate managers and partner sites. In short, they can give you a tremendous boost when it comes to getting coupons on a regular (daily) basis. They also screen to make sure coupons are legitimate (not fakes or copies). Using an affiliate ID in the XML delivery to your site, you can make money from merchant sales without having to track down coupons from a wealth of sources. As of the fall of 2012, CouponFeed had more than 11,000 merchants and more than 34,000 coupons. The cost started at under $15 a month—possibly more for additional features.

Using Brandcaster®, Coupons.com's affiliate program, you can place and customize a coupon gallery on your site. They also offer a means of placing ads for coupons on your website if, for example, you are including a blog or your own products. Visitors can stay on your site and find (and print) coupons from your pages without leaving the site.

Places like CouponFeed or Coupons.com's Brandcaster as well as Smash Deals (smashdeals.com) or RedPlum's (redplum.com) affiliate programs are ways to jump into the coupon field without having to start from square one. For Me to Coupon (www.formetocoupon.com) is another such affiliate site with an automated customized coupon feed. The site was started by Connie Berg, an online discount maven who founded FlamingoWorld.com, which offers discounts and coupons from online retailers, and iShopDaily.com, which focuses on price comparison and product search.

There are a number of other affiliate programs available. However, you need to read the fine print on any affiliate program offered by a coupon or deal site before jumping on board. Affiliate programs can get you started in an extensively crowded coupon industry, but they can also lead nowhere if they are not with a trusted site.

Aggregator Sites

If you are going the route of an aggregator, providing the best deals from elsewhere, you can simply post deals or coupons from wherever you see fit. Most often nobody will stop you. However, you won't make anything for such postings without working a deal with the other site(s) that are posting the deals or coupons. While some of the larger players may not find it necessary to link with you, others will be happy to let you spread the word on their deals for a small commission.

Establishing relationships is, once again, the key to success. YipIt, the leading aggregator, posts deals from Groupon, LivingSocial, Google Offers, Amazon Local, and so forth. The nice thing about running such a site is that you are letting these sites find the deals and work out the terms, while you simply post them and reap some rewards. The negative, as mentioned earlier, is that most aggregators need another revenue stream since their cut of each deal is typically not very big. The other drawback is that sites like Google and LivingSocial email their subscribers like crazy, so there is less need to use your site. On the flip side, you can promote the fact that you are a one-stop shop for many such daily deal sites and you can also lessen the influx of emails in your customers' inboxes.

Summary Points

- *We started the chapter with the four key elements of this type of business:* your network of customers (i.e., your subscriber base), your website, your merchants, and your marketing.

- *There are several ways to make money from a coupon or deal site.* The primary means of revenue, especially for daily deal sites, is through the split with the merchants on the actual deals. Selling ads on your site or working through an affiliate program are also popular means of revenue.

- *Building a subscriber list is essential.* Social media is the primary means of generically growing such a list. Brick and mortar methods are also effective. If you do, however, have access to a list of emails (created through legitimate means), this too can benefit you when starting this type of business.

- *Knowing what you want in your website and having it built to your liking are essential.* There are daily deal and coupon-building platforms that are cost-effective and make life easier so you do not have to reinvent the wheel.

- *In a mobile world, it is also becoming essential to have an app.* But an app needs to link to data, so build up your website and your merchants list first.

- *Prior to seeking merchants, you'll want to have all of your ducks in a row.* This means knowing how you will structure a deal, what your refund policy is, and all of the particulars. Have a contract made up for merchants to sign and ask your lawyer to review it. Then, start looking for merchants in directories, through the chamber of commerce, or from any lists that suit your niche market.

- *Coupons should come from merchants.* Coupon fraud does exists, so make sure you utilize legitimate, ethical, and legal means of obtaining your coupons, such as coupon affiliates like Coupons.com and RedPlum.com.

- *Aggregator sites are those that feature the best of other sites.* You can get a commission for posting deals from other companies.

4

Boring Business Basics
Getting Your Business Started

Okay, so you're all revved up about your upcoming business. Coupons and daily deals are dancing in your dreams. You are salivating at the thought of providing some awesome deals that will dazzle your friends and family! But—and you knew this was coming—you need to get your business basics in order. There are plenty of issues business owners need to address from the start. Getting them in order will allow you to get back to your primary focus: coupons, deals, and discounts!

In this chapter we explore:

- Naming your business
- Licenses and permits
- Zoning laws and other regulations
- Your business structure
- Lawyers, accountants, and insurance agents, oh my!
- Employees
- Uncle Sam

So, What's in a Name?

When it comes to business, a lot.

The name you choose for your business will be with you (hopefully) for years to come—it will be how your merchants and customers know you and will reflect the type of online coupon business you offer. For example, LivingSocial emphasizes the social aspect of savings while Groupon acknowledges that it is a group savings site as well as an easy–to–remember, one-word title, much like Amazon, Facebook, Netflix, eTrade, and eBay. Coupons.com was gobbled up a long time ago on the internet, making the coupon concept as clear and concise as possible. Of course there are also plenty of variations on the coupon concept, such as Coupon Mountain, Coupon Mom, Coupon Searcher, and Coupon Tweet.

What you need today is not just a catchy name, but one that comes up in web searches. The word "coupon" is so widely used that many people are now looking for other keywords in their names, such as "deal" or "save." Slickdeal and Dealfind are easy ways to utilize the word "deal" in an easy–to–remember fashion, much as Eversave and Coolsavings utilize the words "save" or "savings." Names today, especially for an online business in a competitive marketplace, are in part predicated on keywords and search engine optimization (SEO).

If you are planning to run a regional site featuring local deals, you can incorporate your region into the name such as SouthwestDeals, SouthwestSavings, or Kalamzoopons. If you are directing attention to moms, then you can use something similar to DealSeekingMom, MoneysavingMom, or CouponMom. If you have a hook, then use that. eBates, for example, features many online rebates, so they worked that into their name. Some people want to make you feel like they are your bargain

Beware!

Too many websites with the same key-words will bury yours in the pack. If you use the same words (i.e., "coupons" and "deals"), you won't stand out. Instead, try to find a URL that is both memo-rable and unique—one that people can easily bring up and mention in a conversation. You need to find a URL that can carry a brand identity, and is easy to say and spell. If you can find a niche and use keywords that are niche oriented, you can move up in the listings for your target market.

buddy, such as BuyWithMe. You might want to be complimentary and indicate that your customer is making the smart choice with something like SmartSource (although it doesn't really indicate that it is a coupon or "deal" site). Hip2Save lets customers know that they are "hip" to save money.

Of course, you also need to be careful in the name you choose. Not only do you need to do an online search to make sure the domain name is available before committing to anything, you also want a name that doesn't come off as being affiliated with another site or business. TotallyTarget has clear disclaimers indicating that they are in no way affiliated with the store Target. While TotallyTarget does well, it might be easier if you are not at all misleading. The same holds true for CouponingtoDisney.com, which is a site that many people believe has Disney discounts, but is not affiliated at all with Disney. It is in essence a site posted by someone earning money to vacation at Disney.

The Name Game

The best thing to do is start out with a list of names that define what you are doing, whether it is running a coupon-clipping site, a group-discount site, or an aggregate site marketing deals from other sites. Play with keywords and search on a few to see how many sites come up. If you search on the word "coupons," you will get upwards of 692 million results. The word "deals" will top 2 billion, while "group savings" will bring you all the way back down to a mere 375 million. So, see how you can craft the words to meet your needs but set you apart from the mass of competition out there.

Once you have a list, run it by friends and family before you even start looking online to see if any sites with that name come up under .com or .net, which are still by far most commonly used in the U.S. and Canada.

Bright Idea

Note: For a URL that has some potential value for better search results, you can visit Zetetic.com, which lists 28 variables that impact domain val-ues. Zetetic also lets you know the value of the URL if you plan to sell it. You can be sure Coupons.com is worth a heck of a lot!

Smart Tip

Do some research on your name, or names, of choice. A New England gallery owner featuring items made with wood from the Australian outback wanted to name the gallery "Get Rooted." However, those who knew what that was slang for in Australia told him it might not be a good idea in the event you get Australian customers and they spread the word. Check that your name has no other obscure or provocative meaning.

Sometimes a friend or someone you know may help you stumble on the best name, the one that just "clicks." Of course names can be changed. After all, Pepsi started out as Brad's Drink, the New York Yankees were once the Highlanders, the Beatles were the Quarymen, and the musical *Oklahoma!* was originally called *Away We Go!* almost up until opening night. Today, of course, with the trouble it takes to build your following online, it's nice if you can start out with a name you love.

Search For (and Register) Your Business Name

Doing a business name search will help you make sure nobody else has the same name. It also appeases the authorities, such as the I.R.S., which likes to have a name on record with which it can keep track of you. The way you register a business name is not a formalized process, but you should look at the website for your secretary of state to find out the way to handle such registration in your state. If you register for an EIN number for employees, now or in the future, you will automatically have the name you use registered as your business name.

You will also do a Google search to find out if your domain name is being used. These are separate activities since buying a domain name does not register your business, and conversely, registering a business name does not assure you that the domain name will be available. Remember that not all businesses have websites, so you may come up with a name that is not a website but instead a printed coupon distribution service in a magazine or mailed circular. For that reason, you want to do separate searches under both domain business names and brick-and-mortar business names.

You can, as some companies do, have a business name and a website under separate

Smart Tip

If a name has a trademark, you can search for it in the United States Patent and Trademark Office, www.uspto. gov or 1-800-786-9199 (toll-free). You can also check the Thomas Register website at www.thomasnet.com for registered and unregistered trademark names. It's a cross-industry database that includes hundreds of thousands of trademarks and service marks. Network Solutions is another place to look for business names online at www.networksolutions.com.

names, like B & J Associates, which owns wxyzcoupons.com. This will give you some leeway if you want to open another site under the same business name later on. Depending on where your business is located, you'll need to register your DBA name ("doing business as") through either your county clerk's office or your state government. In some states no registration of a name is necessary. Check with your county clerk or visit the Small Business Association's website at www.sba.gov and search for "DBA" or go directly to http://www.sba.gov/content/register-your-fictitious-or-doing-business-dba-name and there you will find a state-by-state directory.

Business Licenses and Permits

To run your business legally, you'll need to get the necessary business licenses for your town, city, and/or state. To determine what you need in your jurisdiction, you should contact your local chamber of commerce, city hall, or county clerk's office to find out about such licensing. Most often business licenses are easy to obtain and do not cost very much. You do have to make a conscious effort to renew such licenses as necessary.

You will also want to find out if you need any permits to run your business. Your local county clerk's office should be able to let you know if there are any permits you may need. Common business permits include an air and water pollution control permit, a sign permit, a county permit, or a health department permit. These are not likely necessary for this type of business.

Zoning Laws and Other Regulations

If you plan to launch your business from home, you should check your area's zoning laws. You can usually get a copy of such zoning ordinances from city hall. Typically the concern about a homebased business centers around customers or clients coming to your home, ongoing deliveries being made to your door, or garbage pickup. Since none of these apply to your business, except perhaps having some office furniture delivered, this shouldn't be much of a problem. You should, however, play it safe and know the laws. Difficulty may arise if you have employees coming and going. While you may start out on your own or with a partner, once three of four people are coming and going from your home on a daily basis, you may start testing the zoning laws. This may mean it's time to expand and find an office space that you can afford. An alternative is having your employees working from the comfort of their homes as well.

Mobile devices have led to several people running a business together from separate locations.

Office Regulations

If you are working from an office space, you will typically need to show your business license to your landlord when signing a lease. After that, it is generally a matter of learning the lay of the land; in other words, what you can and cannot do on the property. This may include a discussion of internet connectivity and any other technology you need to run your business. Some older buildings are still not equipped for the fast connectivity you will require for this type of business. Hours of operation may also be an issue when renting office space. A coupon business needs almost 24/7 access for updating listings and fielding emails, texts, or calls from merchants or consumers. This can usually be accomplished with mobile technology, meaning you won't need access to your office 24/7, but you should look for a location that has some flexibility regarding hours in which you can work. Discuss such late-night and off-hour accessibility. Some business owners will only want their tenants in the building during certain hours.

Co-op Boards, Condo Boards, Homeowners' Associations, and Similar Nightmares

As easy as it may seem to simply set up a computer-based business in a quiet office space in your home, you can run into problems with co-op boards, condo boards, or neighborhood associations. While there are some such entities that do good work for their communities, many such boards and associations are made up of people who do not have enough "power" at their jobs, in their homes, or in their communities. As a result, many join these boards or associations in an attempt to assert some type of power to make themselves feel better about their limitations elsewhere. As a result, they go out of their way to make others miserable if at all possible; sad, but so true.

If you find yourself falling victim to such tactics, see what it is that they need you to do to appease their "concerns." Try hard to keep smiling and be accommodating to keep your life trouble-free. The biggest real issue that may arise will come from adding on employees. While some board members are concerned that almost everyone is a serial killer, the more practical (and valid) concerns center around parking and liability. The latter is also a valid concern for you as a homeowner. The more people in your home, the more likely someone can get injured and the more insurance coverage you will need. Again, this is usually the time—once you start hiring employees to work at your home—to look for an office space.

Know When to Go!

If the following five tips are true for you, it's time to move out of your home office and into an office space:

1. You find you are spending more time on home distractions than on work.

2. You have outgrown your office with equipment and have a printer on your baby's changing table.

3. Your employees are eating you out of house and home.

4. Your neighbors are complaining about your staff's cars blocking their driveways.

5. One of your children starts calling one of your employees "Mom" or "Dad."

Business Structures

While a business name is important, so is setting up the structure of your business. You can operate as a sole proprietorship, a partnership, corporation, or a limited liability corporation (LLC). Your accountant and/or attorney can help you with such a decision. Besides needing to appease those pesky people at the IRS, you will determine your business structure based on several factors including:

- Tax advantages and disadvantages
- Personal and professional liability
- Employees, now and in the future
- Investors

Sole Proprietorship

Most online coupon businesses start out with the simplest business structure, the sole proprietorship. If you'll be starting out on your own, you may choose the same option. It's the least complicated and the least expensive. You can always switch to another structure later on if you take on partners and/or employees. The advantage of a sole proprietorship is that you have little to do: You get a business license and file the necessary business forms applicable within your state, and you are in business. There is very little paperwork and few formalities, other than paying taxes. Your income is reported on your personal or jointly filed tax return.

The disadvantage, however, is that if your business gets sued, so do you, personally. In other words, you are held liable and it can put a serious dent in your personal finances. In a litigious society, it may be more comforting when dealing with such a broad-based business to take greater precautions.

Incorporating

As a corporation, you have more leverage when negotiating with banks by reminding them the corporation guarantees the note. Even though the bank will probably still ask you for a personal guarantee, you can use your corporate status during such negotiations.

The biggest plus for incorporating, however, is that by having the business as a separate entity, you are typically not personally held liable if you are sued for any reason. However, by incorporating you will also have a lot of paperwork and various requirements that you must fulfill as set forth by the state in which you incorporate. There is also the possibility of double taxation when you form a corporation, meaning that you pay corporate taxes, and then when you take money out of the corporation, you pay taxes again on your personal assets. You need to sit down with a business attorney or your accountant and weigh the plusses and minuses of incorporating, as well as how to avoid such double taxation. Most coupon businesses do not start out as corporations.

Limited Liability Corporation (LLC)

A limited liability corporation (LLC) is another option that is somewhat of a hybrid between incorporating and going solo. The advantages of forming an LLC are that the members are afforded limited liability and have pass-through taxes. By forming an LLC, rather than a corporation, you receive nearly all of the benefits of a corporation but avoid some of the drawbacks, such as double taxation as well as some of the requirements of incorporating and the excessive paperwork. Unfortunately, LLCs are not offered in all states.

Partnerships

As for partnerships, proceed with caution. Make sure you have a partnership agreement spelled out detailing who is responsible for which tasks and functions.

Also make sure you determine in advance whether one of you is a silent partner or a limited partner. You will need to have an attorney draw up such an agreement. You'll also need to have very clear guidelines about how the partnership can be dissolved. If you do decide to partner with someone you know and trust (never partner with anyone you do not know well), you can divide up responsibilities. For example, one of you can be seeking out the merchants while the other one is building the website and determining how to effectively market it. Spell everything out in advance and put it in writing.

> **Tip...**
>
> **Smart Tip**
>
> If you plan to partner, explore your skills and those of your partner. Most businesses start out with more than one person and they compliment each other as a lyricist and composer, both with great, but different skills. If you are great with numbers, then you handle the finances and partner with someone who has great ideas for designing the website or perhaps with someone who is great at sales.

Business Structures: Taxes and Liabilities

Taxes

○ *Sole Proprietorship*: Profits and losses pass through to personal income

○ *General Partnership*: Profits and losses pass through to personal income

○ *Limited Liability Company*: Profits and losses pass through to personal income

○ *Corporation*: Corporate income taxes, no pass-through to personal income.

Liabilities

○ *Sole Proprietorship*: Unlimited personal liability

○ *General Partnership*: Unlimited personal liability

○ *Limited Partnership*: Limited personal liability

○ *Limited Liability Company*: Personal liability protection

Attorneys, Accountants, and Insurance Agents, Oh My!

Attorneys are like plumbers—you typically don't think about hiring one until you have an urgent problem. But as a business owner, you should have a good business attorney at the ready from the very beginning, one who knows small business, and preferably one well-versed in the legality of offering coupons or daily deals. You can do your due diligence in all aspects of starting up a business, but having a lawyer also "watching your back" can help, especially in a business that is so rich with contracts and so ripe for illegal activities. As discussed in Chapter 3, "How It Works," there are many coupon scams, so you need to be extra careful in this business.

Not only do you want an attorney to assist you with your merchant contracts, but also in all your legal postings on your website. Running a coupon website means having the finest of fine print so you know exactly what you are and are not responsible for when someone prints and redeems a coupon offer from your site or buys a daily deal from you.

Problems will arise, such as when coupons cannot be redeemed, when daily deals are not honored, or when conditions are not spelled out properly. Sometimes your merchants go out of business, leaving you holding the coupons or the deals. These are potential headaches that your attorney can help you avoid.

Therefore, you will want to find a lawyer who is particularly adept with contracts and understands, or has the ways and means (or staffers) to research, the industry.

Accountants

You will need to discuss your newly founded business with an accountant and determine if he or she can handle the business tax and financial needs. Once you have determined how you will make money, which is typically from commissions, through advertising, or perhaps memberships to the

> ### Smart Tip
>
> **Tip...**
>
> Know your business income at all times. If you are a sole proprietor and the income from your business is going into your personal income, you need to keep excellent records. The IRS will want to know how much income is coming from your daily deal or coupon business, how much is coming from other business activities, and how much is coming from gambling or other sources of income.
>
> Keep good, accurate records if all of your income is going into one place. For this reason, it's advisable to have a separate bank account for your business.

website, you can work with your accountant to best determine your tax situation and your potential business structure.

Factors to discuss with your accountant include:

- Whether or not this is a sideline or a full-time business
- Your sources of revenue from the business
- Whether or not you are hiring people
- How to best protect yourself from liability
- Your current tax situation and what you will need to pay in your state (or city) as well as in federal taxes

Factors to look for when choosing an accountant include experience, particularly with online businesses, small businesses, and startups, and knowledge on the latest tax laws and how they pertain to small businesses and income through commissions, since you typically are not selling products.

Insurance Agents

If you are operating your business from home, discuss with your insurance agent your current policy and let him or her know that you are operating a business. You'll want the peace of mind that comes with knowing that you are covered in case of any loss or damage to your business. Your most valuable assets are your computers and the data in which all of your merchant and customer information are stored.

The bottom line is to think through and make a plan that covers you for anything that prevents you from doing business. That may include stolen or damaged equipment. Check with your homeowner's policy to see whether it covers personal property, such as a laptop computer, that is not actually in your home when damage or loss occurs. Since you may be doing a lot of mobile work as you travel to meet merchants, you'll also want to select an insurance plan that covers portable electronic equipment. More companies today are routinely insuring PDAs, notebook computers, and even cell phones. Calculate how much coverage you need for your laptop computer or other portable equipment. This information can usually be found on insurance websites and rates are relatively inexpensive.

Additionally, you may want business interruption insurance in case a natural disaster or some unforeseen occurrence shuts you down for some time. This is also not typically very expensive.

Also, check with your insurance agent and your attorney to ensure that if someone purchases a daily deal from your site and gets injured from the experience (such as a trip to an amusement park and they fall off a ride), that you are not at all responsible.

Employees

When you start out, you may be on your own or working with a partner. In time, however, you may decide to hire some help in order to better establish yourself, build a following, and attract merchants. In this industry, without a following you're nothing.

As time goes by, should your business grow as you expect, you may need some additional help to manage merchants and update the website, and/or customer service reps for fielding customer questions, comments, or complaints.

Bringing in employees with a knack for deals and an interest in coupons is a plus, but not essential, as you can teach them the fine points.

Employer Identification Number

On the federal level, if you are hiring employees, you will need to obtain an Employer Identification Number, a unique nine-digit number that's often considered a corporate equivalent to a Social Security number. Sole proprietors without employees technically don't need EINs because they can use their Social Security numbers on any business-related forms. Most sole proprietors, however, prefer using an EIN to keep business and personal affairs separate, and to guard against identity theft.

It's easy (and free) to obtain an EIN from the IRS's website. For more on obtaining an EIN, visit irs.gov and search on "EIN."

If your business is headquartered in a state that collects income tax, you will also need to obtain a state employer identification number or charter. Check with your state's treasury department or department of revenue.

The Help You Need

One of the worst things a new entrepreneur can do is hire the wrong people while launching a business. First, you do not have money to waste. Second, you want to get off on the right foot. Therefore, it is imperative that you discuss the specific needs for which you are hiring someone and carefully determine if they have not only the skills, but the disposition and reliability to work hard, on their own (since you won't have time to micromanage) to do the job efficiently. Do background checks, call references, and don't do anyone a favor when starting a business, such as hiring your neighbor's son just because he needs a job, even though he's a pothead. Hire slowly and fire quickly—it may not be the most amiable way to do things, but this is your business, and until you get up and running, you cannot wait for people to adjust or make their way slowly around the learning curve.

Also, before you hire anyone, have set policies in writing. These can range from no sexual harassment to signing a confidentiality agreement to a zero tolerance policy when it comes to showing up drunk. Write down your rules and policies and have employees sign them to protect you from any future lawsuits.

Uncle Sam

Taxes are part of any business, and web businesses are no exception. Following the guidelines set forth by Uncle Sam and the IRS (assuming you can understand them) is part of being in business.

State Tax License

If you're engaged in the sale of goods or services, you'll likely need to obtain a state tax license. The rules vary by state, but generally most sales to customers are taxable, and the government simply finds it easier to make the seller (that's you) collect sales tax.

In this case, while you are NOT "selling" coupons, you may be selling memberships or other products. Talk to your local state tax office about sales tax requirements. When selling daily deals, you are not collecting tax on selling a voucher for a deal. You will, however, pay taxes on income. All businesses must file annual income tax returns, including those that are run on the internet.

As a sole proprietor or partner, or if you have an LLC or S corporation, you will need to pay estimated taxes to the federal government (and possibly your state government) if you expect to owe at least $1,000 in tax for the current calendar year after subtracting your withholding and credits *and* you expect your withholding and credits to be less than the smaller of:

- 90 percent of the tax to be shown on your tax return, or
- 100 percent of the tax shown on last year's income tax return. Your tax return for last year must cover all 12 months.

Quarterly taxes are paid for the calendar year on April 15, June 15, September 15, and January 15. If these dates fall on a Saturday, Sunday, or a federal holiday, the date will be pushed back to the next business day.

If you are filing a tax return for a corporation, you generally have to make estimated tax payments for your corporation if you expect it to owe tax of $500 or more when you file its return. If you work by yourself, you will also pay self-employment tax, which includes Social Security and Medicare tax payments. If you have employees, you will pay employment and payroll taxes.

Statutory Payroll Tax Deductions

Payroll taxes must be withheld from an employee's paycheck. This is required by law. Employers must hand these withholdings over to various tax agencies. Payroll tax deductions include the following:

- Federal income tax withholding (based on withholding tables in Publication 15)
- Social Security tax withholding (6.2 percent up to the annual maximum)
- Medicare tax withholding (1.45 percent)
- State income tax withholding
- Various local tax withholdings (such as city, county, or school district taxes, state disability, or unemployment insurance)

If your online business has employees and has $2,500 or more taxes due in the current or prior quarter, you are required to file Form 941 for payroll taxes (employee income tax withholding, Social Security, and Medicare contributions). You can file Form 941 and make a deposit using the Electronic Filing Tax Payment Service (EFTPS) or deposit coupon on payday or make a month's worth of deposits on the 15th day of the following month.

Independent Contractors

In the course of building your coupon or daily deal business, you might prefer to hire independent contractors or "freelancers" to design your website, help with your marketing strategies, attract new merchants, or perform any of the many duties that come with the territory. It is important to properly classify any independent contractor when it comes to paying taxes. Unlike "employees" for which you will have to pay unemployment tax on wages, you do not pay these taxes nor are you responsible for withholding taxes on payments to independent contractors. They are responsible for their own tax payments.

When you get to the point of hiring employees and/or independent contractors, you will have to determine which are which, for tax purposes. Typically, if someone is hired by you and working regularly for your business on your schedule and on your terms while receiving a steady, weekly salary to work solely for your business, in your business space, with your equipment, he or she is an employee. But if the individual has a business of her own, works for you on her schedule, uses her own equipment, and does other projects for other clients, she is an independent contractor.

You can also use the "right to control" test. This is typically explained by the courts as follows: In situations in which the hiring party controls the way work is carried out and a product or service is delivered, the relationship between the parties is considered to be that of employer/employee. However, should an employer not have authority over how a party accomplishes his or her work, but simply gives an outline, the relationship between the parties is that of hiring party/independent contractor.

To be sure of the difference between an employee and an independent contractor, you can always go to the IRS website at www.irs.gov.

Summary Points

- A good name can be hard to come up with, but once you find one you like, it will be your business identity. So take your time and consider many possibilities. A name can tell people what you do, where you do it, and who your market consists of. It can also help you create and build your brand.

- Today you need to find both a business name and a domain name that are easy to remember and not being used elsewhere. Do a business name search and a domain name search. You'll also want to have "keywords" that might otherwise not bring up the torrents of results found under the words "coupons" or "deals." Select keywords carefully for SEO.

- You will also need to determine which licenses and permits you will need for your business. Zoning laws may apply if you are operating from a home office. Get to know such laws and ordinances in your area and also work within the rules and regulations of any local boards or associations.

- The business structure you choose is important for tax and liability purposes. Discuss the pros and cons of each with your accountant and your attorney before determining which is best for you. Make sure you have an attorney, accountant, and insurance agent at the ready to discuss your various needs.

- Employees can help you start, grow, and maintain your business. Make sure to hire carefully after setting up your guidelines and policies. Don't forget to check references.

- And finally, know your tax situation. It's easy to immerse yourself in business and not think about taxes until it's time to pay them. Plan ahead, know what needs to be filed, and pay your quarterly taxes and payroll taxes in a timely manner.

The Home Office or the Business Office

It's not uncommon for a coupon or daily deal business to start from the comfort of someone's home. After all, most of your business centers around your website and through online communication. Getting started will likely mean reaching people on- and offline to get them to become online subscribers. Typically that does not mean they will be arriving at your place of business.

Meetings with merchants will also commonly occur at their business locations. And your computers and mobile technology will not take up a great deal of space. In short, you can launch your coupon or daily deal business from a homebased office as long as your business needs are met. In this chapter we will discuss:

- Homebased businesses
- Setting up your home office
- Being technically efficient
- The homebased business lifestyle
- Finding an office space
- Leasing your office space
- Office furniture

Homebased Businesses

Starting a business at home was once seen as a glorified hobby, a sideline, or something that was not taken very seriously. That has all changed. In fact, statistics now show that if you start your business at home you have a better chance to succeed. According to the Home-Based Business Institute's spring 2012 statistics,, roughly 70 percent of homebased businesses will succeed in their first three years, compared to 29 percent of other business ventures. This success results in $427 billion earned annually by homebased businesses, which, according to the *Pittsburgh Business Times*, is more than General Motors, Ford, and Chrysler combined.

If these numbers don't get you excited, add in the growth factor in both the coupon industry and daily deal industry. According to the Jupiter Research Group, the coupon industry is predicted to top the $46 billion mark by 2016. Meanwhile, the daily deal industry, according to IBISWorld, is expected to continue in the growth phase up until 2017, giving you plenty of time to get your business up and running.

Setting Up Your Home Office

As a homebased coupon or daily deal entrepreneur, you can set up your office anywhere in the house that's convenient; but ideally, you should have a dedicated office, a room that is reserved just for your business. You can locate this room in a den, a finished room over the garage, the garage itself, in a finished basement, or a spare bedroom. Keep in mind that whatever space you choose will be your workstation and command center.

> **Stat Fact**
> Among the reasons for the staggering success of homebased businesses are:
> ○ A lack of overhead
> ○ Greater flexibility
> ○ Less time spent on commuting and more time on business
> ○ A better work/family balance

If a dedicated office is not an option for you, you can also station yourself in a corner of the kitchen, or in a part of the family room. If you have a boisterous family, however, a cubbyhole in your bedroom is liable to be much more conducive to quiet, clear thinking than a nook in the family room with the TV blaring at all hours.

Remember, this is a business that runs 24/7 since coupons can be printed and deals can be purchased 24/7. Therefore, you may need to be on your computer posting tomorrow's deals or fielding phone calls or emails for answers to various problems. You'll want to plan, starting early on, to have your iPhone, Galaxy, or other mobile device at the ready at all times and have voicemail or a virtual assistant cover for you when you are not available.

Distraction Free

Obviously, running a business means you will need a lot of quiet time to focus on the many tasks at hand. The fewer distractions, the better. Of course, "distractions" is a broad term that means different things to different people. Some homebased business owners work best when music is playing, phones are ringing, and texts are coming in frequently. Conversely, others need to focus intently on each task and want a quiet environment. To each their own.

The point is that you need to find your comfort zone, a place where you can work at your best. For most entrepreneurs, this also means finding a time when the kids are at school, asleep, or with your spouse, significant other, or perhaps at daycare. The point is you need time to think clearly about the many aspects that go into such a business.

Being Technically Efficient

The coupon industry was once all about designing and printing coupons. They were then typeset to appear in print. Today all of that has changed. Everything is computerized. Running an online business means being connected. This means having good cable and/or wifi connectivity at all times. Since your business depends on your connectivity, you need to make sure you also have solid phone connections. A home office in a place that barely gets cellular service is not a good plan.

Computer Specs

Computer systems, including the CPU, monitor, keyboard, and a printer, can be found for under $1,500, and notebooks or laptops for even less than $1,000. Look for something in the mid to high end of the spectrum since your computer is your lifeline. Shop at the major stores such as Best Buy, Apple Stores, or online sites such as Amazon.com. You can also go to the company's websites at HP.com, Apple.com.mac/, Gateway.com, Lenovo.com, Dell.com, and so on. It's advantageous to deal with major name stores, manufacturers, or known websites for warranties and tech support, which may not be as reliable from small shops.

Whether you are planning to buy a computer or intent upon using the one you already have, you should look for the following:

- Minimum 4 GB of RAM, but you're best going for more
- At least 500 GB of hard disk memory
- Computing speed of at least 2 to 3 GHz for laptops (to conserve battery), otherwise 3 to 4 GHz for desktops. Intel I5 or equivalent contains four CPU cores for multitasking.
- USB ports for peripherals, typically four in back and two on the front panel. The newest/fastest standard of USB 3.0 is becoming common.
- A DVD R/W drive, although some laptops leave this out nowadays
- Windows 7 or higher. Unlike the Home version, the Pro version is preferred if you plan to be networking several PCs.
- Internet access by Ethernet hardwired is best. Alternatively, wifi 802.11N was the fastest until recently when version 802.11AC came out. It will go further and faster when more widely available (backward compatible to 802.11G, A and B).
- 3-D graphics card, which will allow you to get the latest software programs and use them to your advantage.
- 5.1 surround sound (not essential for your purposes, but always a plus for quality sound, such as some background music while you're in the throes of your workday).

> ### ⚠ Beware!
> Mobile devices are getting hacked more frequently than ever. Too many people are under the impression that they are 100 percent safe. They are not! Be careful using mobile devices from unsecured locations (such as restaurants) for banking and for sending sensitive business materials. Also, while Macs do not typically get viruses, they can, so be on the safe side by having antivirus protection.

- A firewall and antivirus software. The firewall should be part of your purchasing deal, while antivirus programs are a must today for anyone using the internet for any reason; these often come with the computer package. Make sure to update it often. Also consider Webroot Secure Anywhere and Trend Micro Titanium: These newer antivirus/antispyware programs are continuously updated instead of periodically. Free ones that are pretty good include AVG or Avast.

- Also, you need to have at least an 802.11 N router (which also has four Ethernet jacks) that includes a hardware firewall. Use a router, even if only one PC is attached, since it is safer than connecting directly to a cable modem. Most ISPs now include the wifi router as part of the package.

While some people feel that desktops are the dinosaurs of the modern business world, others like having one around. No, they aren't mobile, but you can get a larger screen and not have to worry about recharging your battery. Many business owners have one of each.

Lighting and Temperature

Good lighting is essential for productivity—and for your eyes. Don't depend strictly on overhead lighting for a lot of deskwork. Lamps can be of great benefit for your desk or workstation. Plus, you can move them around as necessary. As for a comfortable climate, it is no fun working in either the coldest, warmest, or driest part of the house. Too much heat or cold are also not good for technical equipment. Determine where you'll physically be most comfortable, and whether you'll need to invest in additional air conditioning or supplementary heating units (i.e., electric space heater). Controlling your climate is beneficial to your productivity. Good ventilation is also a plus!

Use the handy "Home Office Worksheet" on page 74 to locate and design your home office.

The Homebased Business Lifestyle

Starting your coupon or daily deal business from home may sound very appealing. After all, the business will have you at your computer and/or on the phone most of the time, so an elaborate office is unnecessary. The cost savings of not having overhead by renting office space is also a plus when starting out. Until you outgrow your home office, which will be primarily because you will need to hire employees, you'll do fine as long as you can adjust to the homebased work lifestyle.

Home Office Worksheet

Sure, we are living in a mobile world and you can work from any number of locations, but there's something to be said for having your own comfortable space in which to work. Start by listing three possible locations in your home for your office, which should include a work area for you and enough space to meet your technical needs as well as your office furnishings.

1. _____

2. _____

3. _____

Next, take a physical survey of each location and ask the following questions:

Q: Will your current desk or table (or the one you have your eye on) fit?

_____

Q: Do you have adequate lighting? If not, can you create or import it? Can you work some natural sunlight into your plan?

_____

Q: Is there proper ventilation?

_____

Q: What is the noise (or distraction) factor?

_____

Q: Is there room to spread out your work?

_____

Q: Can all of your technical devices fit and work (laptop, printer, etc.) comfortably?

_____

Home Office Worksheet, continued

Q: Are you going to be freezing or sweating? Remember to think about temperature.

_____

Q: If you are a couple in business together, a partnership, or you have an assistant who will be working with you, is there adequate space for him or her to work comfortably?

_____

Q: (optional) How close is it to the coffee maker? Refrigerator? (This can be either a plus or minus, depending on your current waistline and jitter factor.)

_____

There are a lot of positives about working from home. But there are some negatives, too. Here's a brief overview of the advantages and disadvantages or working at home.

Advantages of Working at Home

For many people, working at home is a blessing. Some of the perks include:

- *Saving significant time on commuting.* Without, for example, a one-hour trip each way to and from an office, you save 10 hours a week.
- *Home comforts including your own kitchen and bathroom.*
- *More time around the family.* However, you need to set some ground rules such as "Please don't disturb me when I'm in my office unless it's really, really important."
- *Some equipment already on hand.* This can be tricky, because you should have a separate computer for work and separate phone lines. However, you may be able to borrow a lamp from the den, a chair from the basement, etc.
- *Low-cost starting point.* If you're starting out and don't want to pay rent for an office, this is a great way to launch a business without much overhead. You can

also save some money by deducting your home business expenses on your tax return.

Disadvantages of Working at Home

- *Losing your motivation.* This is the one disadvantage that destroys many home-based businesses. It's tempting to turn on the TV, or do something else that is fun. You must learn self-discipline and self-motivation.

- *Overworking.* While some people will get easily distracted, others will see the office as a place to spend all of their time, since it's so convenient. If this is you, you'll need to discipline yourself to stay out of the office on occasion so that you can enjoy the rest of your life and not burn out.

- *Loneliness.* Although in this field you will be in constant contact with merchants, your tech and web people, and others, working at home can get lonely. You may miss the companionship and camaraderie found in an office environment. You'll need to take breaks and get out on occasion. Meeting friends for lunch is a great way to break up your day.

- *Entertaining clients.* Should you be meeting in person with a merchant, you will need to meet at his or her place of business—which is common in

Homebased Business Tax Deductions

Remember to take your homebased business deductions on your tax returns. This can include indirect business expenses that apply to the entire house. For example, you can deduct the portion of your rent and mortgage as well as electric, heating, or other utilities that are used for the portion of the house from which you are doing work. Therefore, if 10 percent of the square footage of your home is your office, then you can typically deduct 10 percent of such expenses. Of course there are also direct home office expenses such as the new window treatments necessary to keep your office insulated and your new computer. Be careful, however, to deduct only what you use for business—the IRS is very aware of the increase in home businesses and quite familiar with homebased business deductions, so it's advisable to review all deductions with your accountant. Keep in mind that you can also deduct a percentage of your gas (based on IRS allowable miles) for driving to meet merchants.

the industry—or at a neutral location, such as a diner or a Starbucks. Typically, home businesses are not ideal for entertaining clients.

- *Limited growth potential.* When you suddenly find that you cannot handle the workload of the business yourself and want to bring on employees, this is difficult to do from a home office.

The Virtual Office

Working from home today is largely possible because of the emergence of the virtual office, which has grown in popularity over the past 15 years and continues to grow with the advent of new technology. The virtual office makes it appear to the outside world that you are working from a busy office, when in fact most of your office support is being handled from afar. Nowadays you can utilize the services of a virtual assistant working from their own location while also having voicemail, a post office box, and even tech support (which may also come from your hosting service), all from the comfort of your own home.

Smart Tip

While working from home is a very popular trend, there may still be a stigma attached. Some merchants, working in their shops, restaurants, and various other locations, may not quite realize how productive you may be from your home. Therefore, unless asked, you need not volunteer that you are working from a home base until the merchant sees how effective your deals are. Have an address for your business (your home address) and leave it at that.

Your Office Away from Home

So you don't think you will be motivated to work if you set up a space at home. Perhaps there are three or four of you starting the business as partners and you need one central location that's outside of someone's home. Maybe it's simply a matter of enjoying the energy that comes from getting up and going to your office each day. It could be that you are just too lonely working at home all day, or maybe you want a prestigious business address. These are all among the reasons why some people will want to launch their business in an office space. For others, it's simply more practical from a technical standpoint, while some simply do not have the peace and quiet they need at home.

There's also a matter of growth, and some people anticipate their business outgrowing a home environment too quickly. Whatever your reason, you may be setting up your coupon or daily deal business from an office.

Advantages of Having an Office Separate from the Home

- More space for growth
- Greater opportunity to network in an office building or business area
- A business address looks more impressive
- Fewer distractions
- More workspace and phone lines for sales reps to go after new merchants
- Better for meeting and hiring independent contractors or employees

Disadvantages of Having an Office Separate from Your Home

- Paying rent
- Adhering to a landlord's rules
- Commuting
- Less time with your family
- Parking availability and/or expenses

Your technical needs may dictate your decision. However, if you are starting out, only you can determine the best place to launch your new entrepreneurial endeavor. Clearly, as you can see, there are pros and cons of working at home or at an office.

If you choose the office lifestyle or outgrow your home base, there are several things to consider when seeking an office, such as:

- *How much you can afford to spend on rent.* You will need to factor this into your startup and ongoing operational costs.
- *How far you are willing to commute.* Time spent traveling back and forth to work can cut into your time spent on other tasks, such as marketing or securing deals with new merchants.
- *Accessibility.* Is mass transit nearby? Is parking available? Can anyone find your office, or is it in a remote part of town?
- *The type of office that will meet your needs.* Not working from a home office usually means finding more space so you can hire employees. You'll also need to make sure your communication and technical needs are met. Hint: If you can't get cell phone service, try another location.

- *The neighborhood.* While you may not be able to afford the most luxurious business offices in town, you also do not want to be in an area where you feel unsafe parking or walking.
- *Potential for expansion.* If you lease a small office and your business needs grow quickly, is there room to expand?
- *Restrooms.* Are they safe? Clean? If you see portable toilets, look elsewhere.
- *Security.* You want a building that has a good security system and someone on duty at night, if possible, so you can work at all hours if necessary.
- *Heat and air conditioning.* Make sure you can control it. Note any additional costs.

> **Tip...**
>
> **Smart Tip**
>
> For the sake of having a premium business address and for those who like to get out of their home to work, you can also utilize the virtual office format from a small office location, once again capitalizing on a virtual assistant and professional answering service or voicemail along with remote patching. You can also utilize one of many web conferencing services such as Infinite Conferencing, Cisco Webex Meeting, WatchItToo, or AT&T Connect.

There are a number of options when looking for office space, depending on where you are located. Office parks are designed for businesses to set up shop. The newer ones have the capacities to handle ever-changing technology. They can be advantageous if your business is large and profitable enough to afford what is often a higher rent. Typically you'll also have ample parking and meeting facilities, such as conference rooms, available. Executive suites are also common, whereby several businesses share some of the administrative and other support, such as one mailroom. This can be advantageous if you are sharing with the right business owners. Get to know your office companions and make sure you feel comfortable with the rules and regulations as they pertain to this type of co-op arrangement.

Leasing Your Office Space

It's a big day when you settle into your new office and launch your coupon or daily deal business. But before you post your first coupons or great deal, it's important that you have a lease agreement with which you are comfortable.

As a startup business, you need to be particularly careful since you are the newbie and the landlord has probably offered up many leases to tenants before. With that in mind, never sign anything without having your lawyer take a look.

The first thing you need to do before signing that lease is make sure you have the proper amount of space. Too little space will make life difficult if you anticipate the need for more employees in the short term. Too much space will have you paying for extra square footage that is going to waste. Therefore, it is not only important to know how many people you are anticipating employing, but what they will be doing. In some cases, you will have people writing up daily deals or utilizing their graphics programs from the comfort of their own homes. You may also have marketers out in the field and salespeople meeting with merchants at their places of business. Conversely, you may need some employees in the office helping with the business duties necessary to running a company. It's up to you to determine how much space you will utilize and how much more you may need prior to the end of the lease. Most new businesses today are advised to start more conservatively when it comes to space. If you grow too quickly, you can always have a few people telecommuting.

> **Smart Tip**
>
> In the event that you have more space than you need or a lease that you cannot afford, you can sublease, provided it is agreed upon in the contract. Make sure to look for office space that allows subleasing. Read the fine print that pertains to subleasing very carefully. See the "Questions to Ask When Leasing an Office" worksheet on page 81.

You will also want to see about the length of the lease. It takes a business time to grow, especially in a competitive marketplace where you will need to find new and innovative ways to "out deal" the competition. This can take time and growth can be slow; most businesses do not grow as fast as Groupon. In fact, Groupon was one of the fastest-growing new businesses of all time. Your job is to estimate your growth potential in the space you are looking to lease. The best-case scenario is that you run out of room exactly when the lease is up.

> **Stat Fact**
>
> Businesses that share the cost of the infrastructure can save more than 60 percent on their startup costs and as much as 40 percent on their cost of operations. This means that sharing a reception area, conference rooms, kitchen space, security system, and equipment such as copiers can be very cost effective, provided you are working with a business, or businesses, that have similar needs as yours.

There are plusses and minuses when it comes to how long you want your lease to be: Shorter means if you want to stay, you may have to deal with a rent increase; longer means in the event the business does not take off as planned, or is taking longer than expected to see significant growth, you are still on the hook for more money. You

Questions to Ask When Leasing an Office

First, there is no such thing as a "standard lease," so don't let anyone tell you otherwise. Everything can be negotiated, especially in a building that is not fully occupied. Along with space and cost considerations, you will want to know about the infrastructure of the building.

Below are a dozen questions you may want to ask before you sign a lease for an office space:

1. What type of security does the building provide? This can range from some basic locks or window guards to security surveillance cameras to a security guard. Get an idea of the safety of the premises.

2. Is there someone on call for maintenance emergencies?

3. What additional charges are you responsible for beyond the monthly rent?

4. Are there charges for common area maintenance, such as for the hallways, the lobby, etc.?

5. Are you responsible for paying property taxes, property insurance, utilities, or trash collection?

6. Is there an option to sublease?

7. What fire safety measures are in place?

8. What improvements will the landlord make and what can you do on your own? This could include painting or construction within the office space.

9. Is the building wired for high-speed internet? Very important!

10. What are the policies regarding deliveries?

11. Are you required to purchase liability insurance for your office space?

12. Are there parking rules or restrictions? Some offices may limit the number of vehicles your business can park in their lot or garage.

These are just some of the possible questions you may want to ask before signing a lease. Think of additional ones and write them down in the space provided

Questions to Ask When Leasing an Office, continued

below. You want to make sure all of your needs are covered. You then want to make sure the lease spells out all of these issues. The more answers to these questions you have in writing, the better off you will be.

Additional questions:

_____

_____

_____

_____

_____

_____

will want to factor in your financial backing and see how long you can manage in case the business grows slowly. Just like smaller space is advisable, so are shorter leases in the beginning. You don't want to bite off more than you can chew, or grow too quickly and have space problems.

Office Furniture

Since you are not likely to be entertaining clients from a home office, you can utilize inexpensive furnishings or even use some of what is sitting in your basement, attic, or that which you find at local garage sales. If you are using a desktop, you'll want a computer table and a desk or extended work area to spread out your printed matter. If you are using a laptop, you can improvise, but it is to your advantage to get into the habit of finding a location with good lighting and a good business chair in which you are not slumping, slouching, or doing anything that you will pay for with an aching back later on.

Your home office should not cost much to set up, particularly if you are creative and utilize space wisely. Your office can also reflect your personality, which may make you feel inspired and motivated to get your work done. If you are not comfortable, you will not be efficient. Therefore, try to set up your office and work area with some of the things that inspire you. This can be anything from family photos to collections or hobby items, provided they do not distract you.

An office setup should also be designed in a manner that is comfortable and encourages the workflow. Since you may have others working with you, you will need to determine the best places in which to set them up to accomplish their tasks.

> **Bright Idea**
>
> Climate control can be a big issue in office buildings. Someone will be warm while someone else will be cold. Make sure you find a location with easy-to-control air conditioning and heating. Then try to find a middle ground and maintain a comfortable climate for anyone and everyone. If possible, open windows for cool air to save on energy.

Sales reps, graphics designers, deal copywriters, and any necessary IT folks will all need workspaces that are well lit, quiet, and equipped to meet their technical needs. Copiers, printers, and fax machines can be shared from a central location that doesn't impinge on anyone's work.

Since you may conduct interviews for employees, meetings with merchants, or have your web design team or technical advisors over for reviews or updates, you may want to set up a conference room or meeting space that is cost-effectively designed to be comfortable while aesthetically pleasing.

As for your own furnishings, plan a space that maximizes your productivity. Since most of your day is spent on the computer and/or the phones, have both at the ready with anything else you need within reach. Visualize your office (at home or in an office space), and then make it happen. Also, don't forget to measure your office space as you plan accordingly.

Word of caution: While you will keep most of your data on your computers, it is not advisable to become 100 percent dependent on technology. As long as there are still technical glitches, bugs, and viruses, it's advantageous to have hard copies on file of:

- All contracts
- Your deal offers, vouchers, or coupons
- Your advertising
- Ads placed on your site
- Data about your employees
- Data about your merchants
- Your financial data and records
- Your business plan or outline

You will therefore want to have shelves and filing cabinets included in your office design. While they may not seem "trendy," hard copies are still relevant in courts, at the IRS, and for settling possible disputes.

Summary Points

- It's not uncommon for businesses to start in homebased offices and move out once they grow. This is certainly a low-cost option for this type of business. Determine where you can work at home that is conducive to productivity. Look for a location with few distractions, good ventilation, electric outlets, and one that meets your needs for technology and comfort.

- If, however, you are starting off with a team or do not feel a home office is for you, there are many office spaces you can rent, whether they are in local office parks or in shared office suites. Make sure the space fits your current needs and has some flexibility in the event your business grows.

- Review your lease before you sign it and make sure you can sublet in case you do not need the full space or cannot afford it alone. Remember, leases are negotiable, even if someone tells you that it is a "standard lease." Read it carefully, take notes (since many things are covered in a lease), and discuss the lease provisions with your attorney before signing.

- You do not need to set up a fancy office. Think in terms of practicality and cost-effective efficiency in a home office. If, however, you rent an office space, you may have meetings, so set up a well-planned, comfortable, and aesthetically pleasing conference/meeting room.

Tip...

Smart Tip

"Just find a folding chair or use a chair you already have" is bad advice for someone starting a home office. Hand, wrist, back, and even neck injuries are the results of sitting for hours in the wrong position at your computer keyboard. Many chiropractors and physical therapists are getting rich from such bad advice. For less than $200 you can find a computer chair, and it will be well worth it! Don't skimp on your office chair.

6

You and Your Website

If you are a racecar driver, your most important business ally is your car, and if you are a chef you rely on your cookware and your kitchen. If, however, you run an online business, you are extremely dependent on your relationship with your website. You need to make sure it looks good and meets your customers' needs, while staying away from viruses, hackers, and other technical glitches. This chapter focuses on your all-important partner in this business—your website. We will discuss:

- Hosting servers
- Designing your website
- Landing pages
- Your navigation system
- Testing your site
- Going beyond the basics
- Search engine optimization (SEO)
- Analytics

Hosting Servers

We talked earlier about having a website. What we did not get into are web-hosting servers, which are essentially what puts your website out there for everyone to see. While most humans rarely ever see them, servers are at the core of the internet. Your primary options are shared and dedicated web-hosting servers.

A "dedicated server" means the server is dedicated solely to you. No one else is sharing the server space. This provides you with the best security. Another advantage of a dedicated server is that you will be able to accommodate a large volume of traffic and have more storage. Additionally, you should never have to worry about your site not being up and running 24/7. You can even run several domain names from your own dedicated server. As you might expect, such exclusivity comes at a higher price than having a shared hosting server. For this reason, many smaller businesses start off with shared hosting plans and later move to dedicated servers.

A shared hosting service is one with a number of users running their websites on servers shared with other businesses. You are given a control panel by the service to make the changes to your site. Cost is the main advantage of a shared server, and you will receive plenty of bandwidth for your site. The downside is that there can be security issues with others using the same server—although this is not common—and there may be times that the server becomes overloaded, which may mean you may be "down" on rare occasions. Shared servers typically guarantee that you will be up and running 99 percent of the time.

Leading dedicated hosting services include: SingleHop, Brinkster, Reliable Hosting, and HostGator. Among the many leading shared hosting services, you'll find inMotion Hosting, Web Hosting Hub, GreenGeeks, FatCow, and HostGator.

A couple of great places to look for both dedicated and shared hosting are WebHostGear.com and WebHostingTop.org.

Criteria to look for in a company when looking for web hosting include:

Stat Fact
According to WebHosting.info, as of October 2012 the top web hosting companies in the United States were: WildWestDomains.com with 33.6 million total domains (42 percent of the market), followed by ENOM.Com with 3.2 million domains, NetworkSolutions.com with just over 3 million web domains, 1and1.com at 2.8 million web domains, and HostGator.com at 2.1 million web domains.

- *Reliability and uptime* (meaning how often the server is working properly): Not even the services guaranteeing 100 percent uptime can really be positive that nothing could ever happen to shut them down. That being said, you want a server with the capacity to be up and running as close to 24/7 as possible. In this day and age, it is not that hard to find such reliability.

- *Speed*: The faster the better. Slow-loading pages will kill your conversion rate, which is the rate at which subscribers convert their visits to your site to actual transactions.

- *Reputation*: What are people saying about the company?

- *Features*: Like most anything else today, you can find a slew of features offered by a web hosting company. Don't spend more money on features you don't need.

- *Support*: You want to know that someone is available to help you promptly when necessary.

When looking for a web hosting company, do a little scouting around and even ask other people which companies they use. Remember, you are building a business website that you are hoping will handle a lot of traffic, so look for people who are also using their websites for business. Ask them about their experiences, especially with tech support. You can also go to web forums such as WebHostingTalk.com or WebHostingForum.com and read the postings of others or ask questions.

Designing Your Website

Whether you are using a web design program, online platform, or hiring a web designer, you'll need to know what you want your website to look like before getting started. Looking at other daily deal, membership deal, or coupon websites will give you some ideas of what you do and do not like.

Design

Consider what you need from your design. Remember, you want to design your site to be:

- Easy to read
- Easy to navigate
- Visually appealing
- Easy to share deals
- Adaptable to mobile devices

Coupon Site Design

For coupon sites, bright colors tend to give the site a light and friendly look. The coupons, which are most often provided from merchants, affiliates, or elsewhere, need to be front and center so the product photo (which attracts the most attention), the name of the product, and coupon details are clear. Nobody wants to have to look around to find out how much they are saving or when the deal is over. It is also better to include buttons rather than text links—they stand out.

The rest of the main page will depend on how you want your visitors to find more coupons. You can have links set up so visitors can sort by store names, manufacturers, types of product, top deals, holiday specials, or any other categories you like. Remember to keep it simple so navigation remains easy. If you have free shipping coupons, put them in a category. Your site needs to feature what you have to offer and provide easy access and redemption.

Then there are advertisements. They, too, need to share prime space on your site, especially since someone is paying you to post them. Consider them in your layout. While you want a busy front or main page, you do not want it to be cluttered to the point where people give up and go elsewhere. Therefore, divide it into sections and conquer. People will appreciate knowing where they will find things each time they come to your site—a consistent layout provides a sense of trust so that visitors feel comfortable that they will be able to find what they are looking for.

An Online Example from RedPlum.com

RedPlum.com, a leading coupon site, has coupons on the left side of the page where you can scroll to find plenty. There is a box on the right in which to sign up for weekly coupon alerts, with advertisements beneath it. On top there is also a graphic image relating to the four blogs/articles about savings and finance that you can click on. A navigation bar at the top provides access to grocery coupons, drugstore coupons, restaurant coupons, etc. You can also find (above that) a way to sign on with Facebook, and information about RedPlum's clip-free service is also found in small print on the upper right. Note that on each coupon is an opportunity to forward it to a friend, like it on Facebook, tweet about it on Twitter, or pin it on Pinterest.

Scrolling all the way to the bottom of each page, you'll find some of the web standards:

- Home
- Privacy Policy
- Terms of Use
- Contact Us
- Free Newsletter Sign Up
- Site Map
- Frequently Asked Questions

Note: Most websites also include an "About Us" page providing a brief overview of how the site came to be and when. Also, many sites include a section on how to use the site.

Whether you use an existing template or design your pages from scratch, you can easily sit down with a pencil and paper and sketch out some possible layouts.

Printing Coupons

When visitors find coupons on your site they will want to print them unless all of your coupons are redeemable online. Coupon-printing software is provided by most coupon websites with a simple download that visitors only need to use once. The software is designed to help control the number of coupons that are printed. You will need to provide a brief explanation of the printer software, which is typically downloadable for Mac or PCs. Keep it simple and easy to download.

Daily Deal Site Designs

It seems so easy—you post some great photos of offers with short headlines, include how much your customer is saving and a place in which members can sign up and provide their area code so you can localize their deals.

As LivingSocial does, you can offer some categories such as:

▲

- All deals
- Activities
- Families
- Food and drink
- Health and beauty
- At home
- Nationwide deals

For niche sites, it's advised to include categories that fit your niche market. Many deal sites include getaways and vacations as popular categories. Looking at Gilt, Groupon, LivingSocial, or even Yipit, an aggregator site, you'll see that the lure is the presentation of tempting deals. Influential imagery can make a big difference in promoting your deals. People like to see what they are buying, and the tastier, more scenic, more exciting, more titillating it looks, the more the visitor will be inclined to hit the "buy" button.

Not unlike coupon sites, you will want to be consistent, although deal sites often have little more than the deals spread out on the pages. Make them large enough to attract attention, but small enough to fit a few offers on the screen at any given time. You can utilize categories or, not unlike Yipit, have a variety of offers in plain sight.

Landing Pages

The key to landing deals are landing pages. That's where your customer goes from thinking about the deal to learning more and possibly buying it. Probably the site that best exemplified the concept of great landing pages is Amazon, which still remains the king of such pages. But the daily deal sites are quite impressive. Once your potential customer has shown an interest in a deal and clicks on it, your landing pages are where you can make the sales happen. "Buy Now" should be an immediate (and very simple) option for those who saw the photos and the deal and need not know anything more.

Tip...

Smart Tip
You want to bring a sense of urgency to your deals, and adding a countdown timer can accomplish that, letting your visitor know how much time is left. Some sites use countdowns while others just put down the number of days remaining to cash in on the deal. You can also achieve the sense of urgency by counting down how many seats, widgets, vacation vouchers, or products are left. You want that sense of "buy now."

However, most people like a little foreplay before closing the deal, and this is where you provide the necessary details to pull everything together while making whatever you are selling sound even more enticing. This means you either brush up on your copywriting skills or read a hundred landing pages from other sites and give yourself a crash course in copywriting. You can also hire a copywriter to write about your deals for you—and pay them fairly since this is the lifeblood of your success.

Example #1: PlaySoccer

Headline: PlaySoccer Offers Two Weeks of Outdoor Clinics

Landing Page:

> Wanna get your kids away from their computer games and outdoors playing soccer? Now you can send them to PlaySoccer in one of five great locations in the Phoenix area. Many college players have started at these well-run facilities that feature professional coaches in a safe environment. Pay $16 (regularly $40) for two weeks of Monday, Wednesday, Saturday clinics in April for pre-schoolers (ages 3 to 5).

> For kindergartners through third graders, you can get thorough skills and leadership coaching when you pay $23 (regularly $50) for the Soccer Stars of Tomorrow clinics, which run on Tuesdays and Thursdays.

> PlaySoccer focuses on building skills, confidence, and having fun.

Below this you can include the fine print details as necessary. You'll also want to make sure every deal is easily forwarded to a friend, tweeted, or liked on Facebook. Include directions and add a local map or link to Google Maps or, MapQuest.

See the example on page 93.

Example #2: XYZ Yoga

Headline: XYZ Yoga Offers Five Classes for the Price of Two

Landing Page:

> No, you need not be able to twist yourself into a pretzel to enjoy the health and stress-releasing benefits of yoga. At XYZ Yoga you can enjoy five classes for only $38 (a regular price of $95). In a spacious brand-new state-of-the art studio, you'll be immersed in the ancient art of Yoga while learning over 20 poses plus

breathing exercises that will have you feeling fit, fabulous, and fatigue-free when you leave. Skilled professional instructors guide new students through the basics during Flow Fundamentals sessions, while more advanced students can step into Second Level classes. XYZ Yoga has been written up in *Vantage* and *Yoga Arts* magazines. Ninety-minute classes are given nightly at 7:30 for beginners on Wednesdays and Fridays, and for advanced students on Tuesdays and Thursdays.

Below the copy you can add the fine print, such as:

- Limit one voucher per customer
- All classes must be redeemed by same customer within 30 days of first visit
- Appointments are required and class space is subject to availability
- Merchant cancellation/rescheduling policy of 24 hours applies; voucher subject to forfeiture
- Not valid for customers who have taken a class at XYZ within the previous six months
- If class is cancelled or full, the promotional value of the voucher is good through this deal site for another purchase within one year.

See the example on page 94.

Your Navigation System

One of the keys to a good website is easy navigation. It can make or break your business success. People do not want to jump hurdles to find what they are looking for—so if the navigational system is poor, your conversion rates will suffer. Using an easy-to-read navigation bar or panel on top, or along the side of the page, can make it easy for your visitors to find what they want. Make sure it links exactly to what they are looking for. Poor navigational systems will dump visitors in the middle of a page and make them look further for what they want—they won't do it, so you will lose them. The navigation bar should be in the same place on every page and should always allow them to return to the homepage.

Smart Tip

Tip...

A site map and/or a way to search your site by a keyword are ways to make navigation easier for your visitors. The easier you can make it for them to get what they are looking for, the more conversions you will see.

PlaySoccer offers
2 Weeks of Outdoor Clinics

SAVE MORE THAN 50%OFF   **BUY NOW!**

THE DEAL

Wanna get your kids away from their computer games and outdoors playing soccer? Now you can send them to PlaySoccer in one of five great locations in your area. Many college players have started at these well-run facilities that feature professional coaches in a safe environment.

Pay $16 (regularly $40) for two weeks of Monday, Wednesday, Saturday, clinics in April for pre-schoolers (ages 3 to 5).

For kindergartners through third graders, you can get thorough skills and leadership coaching when you pay $23 (regularly $50) for the advanced clinics which run on Tuesdays and Thursdays.

The PlaySoccer focuses on building skills, confidence and having fun.

THE DETAILS

- Expires Feb 28, 20XX
- Limit 2 players per family.
- See the rules that apply to all deals.

XYZ Yoga Offers Five Classes for the Price of Two

BUY NOW! »

THE DEAL
No, you need not be able to twist yourself into a pretzel to enjoy the health and stress releasing benefits of yoga. At XYZ Yoga you can enjoy five classes for only $38 (a regular price of $95). In a spacious brand new state-of-the art studio, you'll be immersed in the ancient art of Yoga while learning over 20 poses plus breathing exercises that will have you feeling fit, fabulous and fatigue-free when you leave.

Skilled professional instructors guide new students through the basics during Flow Fundamentals sessions while more advanced students can step into Second Level classes. XYZ Yoga has been written up in various health magazines. Ninety minute-classes are given nightly at 7:30, for beginners on Wednesdays and Fridays and for advanced students on Tuesdays and Thursdays.

THE DETAILS
• Expires Feb 20, 20XX
• Most complete all lessons within 6 months
• Limit 1/person, may buy 1 additional as a gift.
• See the rules that apply to all deals.

You also want to think through the visitor's experience on the site. What are the most frequent pages that they visit? Make easy links to these pages so they do not have to go through your homepage or other pages to get there. People don't want to click more than once (maybe twice) to find what they want. And don't forget to make it easy to "Buy" or "Order" at any time. This should be streamlined to utilize only the necessary information so they can check out quickly. You should also have their information stored so they do not need to re-enter it every time they visit your site. Go to Amazon for an example of fast, accurate, and easy checkout. You can find and buy an item on Amazon in five minutes while walking down a crowded street—it's that simple.

Also, make sure your navigation system works with different browsers and on various mobile devices. Therefore if, for example, people do not have JavaScript, have an alternative facility available so they can use the site.

> **Tip...**
>
> ### Smart Tip
>
> Be accessible. There is a tendency in the new "transparent" world for some websites to do everything possible to remain anonymous. If the numbers game is in your favor and people are getting what they need with only a few angry customers, you can get away with it—but keep in mind that a lack of transparency and/or customer service can come back to bite you, especially in an age when bad consumer experiences, or reviews, can go viral. Have a means of contacting your site and a means of getting customer service if you really want to outlast competitors with the "I don't care about my visitors" attitudes.

Testing Your Site

Building a website takes time. For some that means months, and for others it means years. The size and complexity of your site will factor into how long it takes until you launch. Some site owners do a soft launch in an effort to put something up to build their subscriber base.

Regardless of how long it takes to get your site up and running, it is imperative to test everything before launching, and re-test often after launching. In fact, you should be testing your site on the latest versions of Internet Explorer, Firefox, Opera, Safari, Netscape, and Chrome. Remember, people use a wide range of web browsers and you cannot assume that your website will show up as you would like it to on all of them. You will also need to see how your site looks on mobile devices, particularly on iPhones and Androids.

If you want to boost the possibility that your website will work on future versions of all web browsers, you should consider validating the code for your web pages. What this means is that your HTML and CSS are free of syntax errors. Free validators can be found online to do the work for you, pointing out errors in the code and how to fix them. If you are stumped, and there is no automatic fix, you'll need to get some tech support assistance.

You also want to test your links (and, most significantly, your "Buy" button) to make sure that visitors can get to wherever they are looking for. Links should be tested often, especially since you are making changes frequently.

Going Beyond the Basics

Okay, so coupon sites need attractive coupons and deal or daily deal sites need enticing offers. Aggregator sites and affiliates need the same thing, but have much of the offers already designed for them.

However, once you get past the myriad of site necessities from coupons or deals to landing pages to the "about us" pages and the all-important privacy policy (get an attorney to review your policy), there are other possibilities such as blogs and/or articles about saving money or about the niche that your site features.

A number of sites feature blogs to boost their audiences and increase membership—which subsequently makes it easier to get both merchants and advertisers. A blog needs to be well crafted and well written to provide readers with a "takeaway" from the site, meaning some information that benefits them.

For example, you might provide tips on shopping for technology or how to get the best family deals from stores like Costco and BJ's, or tips on greener shopping. Whatever the angle, provide content that is informative and talks to your audience in language they understand. Try to avoid using jargon while also being careful not to talk down to your readers. While personal anecdotes can help make a point, most readers are interested in saving money and not on your personal life.

Along with your own blogs, you can also get guest bloggers to write for your site.

Stat Fact
Web stats show that among the best ways to draw repeat visitors are: using videos (particularly those that are viral), interesting graphics, contests, blogs, surveys, quizzes, relevant trivia, and appropriate humor—not necessarily in that order. Remember, you want people talking about your site and always forwarding anything they like to a friend.

Anyone with a product or service to promote is usually happy to write a little about their area of expertise or let you interview them to write the blog so that it is in line with what your audience expects. Be careful that blogs don't sound like long ads.

Search Engine Optimization (SEO)

The tiny little people running around in the virtual world have a way of finding sites that are "optimized" to be more easily found during web searches. Today, if you want to grow your business, you'll need to optimize your website to come up higher in the search rankings in the seemingly endless array of coupon and/or deal sites.

Therefore, you'll need to play the SEO game, with hopes of being ranked higher on Google, Yahoo!, Bing, and other search engines.

In recent years, SEO had taken on a life of its own. There are books, webinars, seminars, courses, and even rumblings about an SEO college that will teach the never-ending techniques, tactics, and tricks involved in SEO. The problem, however, is that SEO is a system by which the search engines use certain criteria to rank websites, and such criteria can change, making your SEO methodology dated. In fact, too much optimization can work against you, as the search engines get wise to the same old tricks, tactics, and techniques that you (and millions of folks) are using.

With that in mind, it is best to start simple with keywords. These are the words that will draw people to your site. They are taken into account by all search engines. Therefore, you want to choose keywords wisely to separate your website from others. If you are looking for help selecting keywords, you can go to Google AdWords Keyword Tool, Google Insights for Search, Keyword Country, or Hitwise to get an idea of the popularity and success of keywords.

When choosing keywords:

- Start with the obvious, then move on. "Coupons," "deals," "daily deals," "savings," "discounts," etc. should be there, but look for combinations of these overused terms with something else like "Albany deals" or "Iguana food coupons."

- Branch out to more specific terms that will get you noticed: your location, terms that fit your niche market, and so on.

- Think local: Use local words and phrases to attract people in your area.

- Use three- to five-word phrases rather than just individual words, such as "Deals on sporting goods."

- Mix it up: Think about words that accompany different types of deals rather than just different ways of saying "discounts," "savings," or "coupons."

- Include keywords in your meta tags, which are those little tags you see when you scroll across a word or phrase on the page.

You can then put keywords in many places on your site, including blog posts, the "about us" page, and even in the instructions on how to use your site. That being said, the most visited page of your site will be the deals, so you will certainly want to have some of your keywords on that page.

Search engines also look for backlinks from other websites. Try to get reciprocal

Beware!

Search engines can pick up on keywords being scattered about for the sake of it. Too many people have tried (awkwardly) to saturate their web pages with keywords. The search engines have caught on. They can ever penalize you just as easily as they can move you up in the rankings. Don't try to outsmart the system—many before you have tried and failed.

links with merchants, manufacturers, and any other sites you can. Obviously a major company link carries more weight than just linking to your friend's Facebook page.

More traffic is also a means of moving up in the search engine ranking, so try to get as many people as possible to visit your site.

Analytics

You need to keep score, so to speak, when you have a coupon or daily deal (or any type of) website. Analytics can provide you with a wealth of important data for running your deals and marketing your website to your target audience. Google Analytics has become extremely popular, offering users data on up to 10 million hits per month for free. Yahoo!, Adobe, and plenty of software providers can also help you with analytics.

Crazy Egg (www.crazyegg.com) offers analytics and includes Heatmapping, which are reports that let you see what's hot and what's not, so you can make changes that increase your conversion rate of visitors to customers. The goal is to learn where visitors to your site are coming from and what they are doing on your website. You want to get a feel for what coupons or deals are getting the most looks, and which are failing to generate attention. You can also determine what price points are they looking at the most and which search terms or keywords resonate with prospects and lead to conversions. Knowing the most successful keywords that draw people to your website is important for future planning.

Analytics are important for most websites, but particularly in a competitive field in which you want a steady flow of traffic. They can help you determine what to feature on the page based on where your hits are coming from.

Marc Horne at Daily Deal Builder highly recommends that you have analytics in place from day one, because you can also use it to make decisions based on the responses you get. "For example, people will ask us what we think of a domain name or a design layout, or an offer, and it's hard to respond because nobody really knows the answer until you test it and get some numbers," he says. "If you do what is called a 'split test' on your site with version A and version B (of a design, layout, or even copy), you can see what works best. So we always recommend that our clients have good analytics, do split testing, and always focus on increasing those conversion rates."

Beware!
Having analytics but not studying or utilizing them is a waste. Sure, they may be inexpensive, or even free, but if you don't take the time to study them, you may be missing out on some important trends. Don't become negligent (or stubborn) when it comes to using analytics to guide you in improving your website and, subsequently, your business. You can be sure that your competitors are studying their analytic data.

Summary Points

- The type of web hosting is up to you and depends on several factors, including price and security concerns. Consider the pros and cons behind using a dedicated server and a shared server.

- Site design is very important. You need to map out exactly how you want your site to look and be consistent in where you place your coupons, deals, ads, etc., so visitors know where to look. Using RedPlum as an example, we discussed what is typically found on such a coupon site. It is also imperative that you lay-out your pages carefully so that as your coupons or deals change, it will be easy to plug them into the right place.

- Navigation is very important since visitors to your site do not want to waste time on a site that is too slow or too complicated. People will not jump hurdles to find something on your site—they will simply look elsewhere. Your offers should be clear and your buy buttons easy to find.

- Great landing pages can increase your bottom line since this is where your visitors go from browsing to buying. Some samples of headlines and landing page copy were included on pages 93–94.

- Testing your website, including the links and the appearance on mobile technology, is vital. It is also important to think about what else you can put on your website to stand out from the crowd. For example, you could have a blog or another means of grabbing attention with polls, surveys, contests, etc.

- Search engine optimization (SEO), which has become a huge aspect of website success, puts an emphasis on finding the best keywords or keyword phrases to move your website up in the search rankings.

- Analytics is how you find out what is and is not working on your site. You can learn which pages visitors are going to as well as which ones are generating sales and which pages are not. New York City's former mayor Ed Koch used to always ask, "How'm I doin'?" Analytics are the tools that tell you exactly how your website is doing so that you can plan and adjust accordingly.

7

Strategizing with Your Merchants

The most significant relationships are the ones between you and your merchants. You not only need to attract them so they will place their discounts on your website, you also want to establish a rapport so that they return again and again. This means providing them with a good deal and great visibility on your site to help them achieve their goal of increasing business.

▲

Running a successful deal or coupon site means more than just signing up merchants, especially when merchants have so many choices of where to place their deals or coupons. You need to understand how such promotions affect their businesses. Once you do, you can help by discussing and advising merchants before they make a deal—after all, if their deal does not work, they may blame you. If you can provide a "personalized" approach, much like travel agents who continue to outsell many of the cheaper, buy-at-your-own-risk travel websites, you will be able to make a dent in a busy industry.

In this chapter we will discuss:

- Guiding your merchants, or how to help them strategize through each phase of the deal, planning, preparation, managing the deal, and following up
- True stories of merchants who had positive experiences
- The flip side, or negative experiences
- Learning from others' experiences

Guiding Your Merchants

Providing some guidance by educating your merchants can earn you a consulting title, enhancing that which you offer as a business owner. There is a lot that merchants need to know, and while many have had positive experiences, as evidenced by some of their stories in this chapter, many have also learned through trial and error. For example, many restaurant owners, as well as other business owners, learned the hard way how important it is to have enough staff and enough products available. Others leaned that you can't give away too much in the hope of getting return customers. And some learned that you can't sell 200 seats if you only have 100 available. Even manufacturers have learned that putting "while supplies last" on a coupon saves them many headaches.

Planning

Before making any arrangements or signing any agreement, a merchant should

> **Smart Tip** *Tip...*
>
> Encourage business owners to run deals for slower times of year. If your merchant's business is seasonal and customers will pay full price during the busy season, there is no reason for them to run a half-price deal. But if it is shortly before, or after, their peak season, this may be the time to bolster business with a half-price deal or a coupon. Products may also be seasonal. This is why, starting the day after Christmas, stores have been discounting Christmas cards for years. Help your merchants think seasonally.

know his or her goal for running a deal or coupon. The merchant needs to consider the following possibilities:

- Is it to introduce new customers to the business so they will return?
- Is it to introduce a new product or service with the hope that it will catch on?
- Is it to draw customers to the business with a loss leader, to then upsell them on other products or services?

Once the merchant has an idea why he or she is running a deal, the next step is to do the math. A business can handle a loss leader, but if it's bordering on running the owner into bankruptcy, the deal will be too risky.

You can sit down with merchants and help with the math to determine how much they can afford to spend and how much they

> ## Smart Tip
>
> Work with your merchants closely. For example, a restaurant owner may want to sell a $60 dinner for two for $30. He or she will only make $15 when all is said and done. Therefore, you can help the owner decide which items to include in the offer based on the markup costs involved. If the actual food is only $15, he or she is not losing money. And, if you are flexible and work an offer in which they get to take in 70 percent and make $21, they are earning some money, as are you. This becomes a win-win situation and you gain a merchant who will stay with you long term. This is an example of how you can consult with merchants to make the deal work for everyone.

will make. Markup on products is very important to their calculations. This is an area in which you can help them choose the larger markup items to discount. It's also an area in which service providers and merchants selling seats or tickets to an event often drop the ball. A service provider can decide that his or her service is worth $100 per hour and that a great discount is $50 per hour. That is wonderful if such a service is in demand. If, however, people think $50 an hour is still a high rate, it comes down to how much time the service provider wants to be busy. If he or she lowers the rate to $40 an hour and books a full schedule, then there is more money to be made than having a half-full schedule, even at $50. Plus, the more people who utilize the service, the more likely the merchant will gain regular customers. Knowing how much a service is in demand and at what rates people will spend is very important. You can help the merchant do a little research.

Of course, the service provider needs to factor in any costs before making such a decision. Once he or she fills the schedule, the price can be gradually raised. If, for example, the service provider is offering spa treatments, they need to determine how many treatments are possible in the time of the deal. For example, if they can handle 10 treatments a day, then the maximum is 60 for a six-day business week, assuming they have nobody already booked. Some daily deal business owners do not explain such maximums and run a deal in which they sell 500 spa treatments. The deal site owner makes money taking half of each deal sold, but the merchant is well overbooked and loses his or her reputation and possibly the entire business.

This is not the way to run your business, because your reputation for destroying someone else's business will likely come back to haunt you. It is very important that merchants do not try to oversell and that you help them set such caps.

Merchants selling seats to an event or space in a club also need to understand that unfilled seats or empty space on the dance floor is a loss of money. Every time a tour bus leaves or a show starts with empty seats, revenue is lost. Therefore, the goal of a theater, club owner, or dance studio manager is to find price points that will draw enough business to fill the house while still covering expenses. If a dance club holds 200 people, filling the house with 200 people at $20 is $4,000. Having only 75 people at $40 is only $3,000.

In short, merchants need to mathematically figure out the cost factors and possible profits in conjunction with why they are running a deal. You can advise and make yourself a trusted ally rather than just a sales rep looking to sign people up regardless of whether or not a deal is helpful.

> **Smart Tip**   *Tip...*
>
> One thing many merchants do not focus enough attention on is bringing customers back. Here, you might suggest that they offer their own smaller discount for return customers, such as a free appetizer on their first return visit. A $10 appetizer that only costs the owner $4 is worthwhile, since it brings the customer back at very little cost. Help merchants find ways to bring customers back or even suggest an incentive to get their friends to take part in a deal.

Preparation

After the initial planning, and once the discount is in place, whether it is a daily deal or a coupon, merchants need to move from planning to preparation. Again, you can help them.

One of the biggest catastrophes for merchants running discounts or coupons has been not having the manpower to deal with the additional customers. You should discuss this potential problem that has hurt other businesses immensely. Additional manpower is not only necessary for the first few days of a deal but also for the last couple of days when deal or coupon holders realize this is their last chance to get the savings.

Having more employees on hand only solves half of the potential problem. The other half is making sure that the staff knows what is going on. Amazingly, one of the biggest disasters in offering coupons or deals is having employees who have no idea that such a program is going on. Remind merchants to take some time to get everyone up to speed on what they will be handed by customers, including the guidelines and the expiration date. Everyone should be on the same page—it's amazing how many businesses are many pages apart when it comes to such preparation. Staff should not only know about the promotion but also what the goal is. Therefore, they should be upselling items or trying to entice people to return.

Not only does the staff need to be ready to go, but the technology needs to be adjusted to handle any new coupon codes that may appear. Also, it's one thing to say on the coupon or deal voucher "while supplies last," and another to run out of those supplies the first day. Having a weeklong coupon for batteries and running out of them in one day does not does not sit well with customers. Make sure to remind merchants to stock up. Whoever does their ordering has to be prepared.

Managing the Promotion

After planning and preparation comes managing the promotion. Merchants should be trying to win over new customers while also trying to get them on their mailing lists. At spas, restaurants, or other locations where services are provided, you may recommend that they offer a card on which they can review the service and leave some contact information (particularly their e-mail addresses). As an incentive, the merchants might have a drawing to win a free massage, a dinner, or something of value to their customer.

Beware! People sometimes test the waters once they have received something free. They simply want more! While quality customer service is essential, remind merchants that they have to be careful. If word gets out that anyone who complains gets something gratis, a lot more bogus complaints may be sent to the merchant, or to you. The merchants need to be careful when handling such situations. You also need to determine in advance what your policy will be regarding complaints.

Merchants can also offer rewards programs, which provide a great way to get the basic contact information about customers and also encourage customers to return. You should also offer rewards programs for steady customers.

In addition, it's important to remind managers that they need to be on the lookout for fraudulent coupons or vouchers.

Follow-Up

One of your most significant tasks is to sit down with the merchant and review how the discount went. Merchants should be able to learn from what went right and what went wrong, and you can help them reshape the program for the next time. It is important that merchants review whether or not:

- They met their objectives (return customers, increased sales of other products, more new customers, etc.)
- The deal was either profitable or at least not a disaster
- They want to try such a program again

Flexibility Counts

From your standpoint as an entrepreneur, it is important to be flexible within your guidelines. Yes, you want them to provide the details so you, or your copywriters, have enough time to write up something for the website. No, you don't want to lose merchants over rigid deadlines. You may use a prepared sheet so they can fill in the important details of the deal, making it easier to gather the data.

Most merchants would like to at least see the copy before it is posted. One of the two largest daily deal sites allows them to do so while the other does not. As a smaller new deal site, it is in your best interest to show them the copy and permit some changes for accuracy, but not rewrite everything. You should have guidelines in place for the type of graphics you require so that deals look good and stand out. Again, be flexible and help guide your clients in the right direction. Visual images are very important to sales.

Study what your competitors are using and what catches your eye. Ask friends for their opinion on what they notice on a deal or coupon site. To guide merchants, you need to do your homework and learn how to write copy (or hire someone) while also getting a feel for what images are more effective than others.

You can also set minimums when it comes to how much of a discount they must provide, but you also should be flexible on how much you are getting. The major players will ask for 50-percent discounts and then take 50 percent from that total. If it is in your best interest to take 40 percent in order to secure more merchants and help them succeed, then that may be a better option.

True Stories

What better way to learn about deal experiences than to hear it from some merchants? These are a few accounts from merchants who have used daily deal programs.

Moonlight Meadery
in Londonderry, New Hampshire

When Michael Fairbrother left his COO position in a computer software company to turn his passion for winemaking into a full-time career, he knew he was taking a gamble, but hoped for the best. "I started making wine out of my garage in 1996 and began taking it to parties. People seemed to love it . . . they were knocking each other over to get it," says Michael of his early days in the wine business. By 2010, Michael had launched Moonlight Meadery in New Hampshire, roughly an hour from Boston.

About a year into the business, Michael decided to run an offer through a major deal company. The question was: What kind of offer would make good business sense? Selling mead wine and giving free tours of his brewery were the primary aspects of the business. "The rep from the deal company suggested giving away a free bottle of wine, but that didn't make much sense to me because the deal folks would be benefiting but I would be getting only some promotion, which seemed costly," explains Michael.

It was then that the discussion began about creating a value proposition centered on the tours, which he had been giving for free. Having realized the other wineries, such as the ones in the wine country of Northern California, all charged for tours, Michael decided he could charge $15 for his tour, from which he would get $7.50 with the rest going to the daily deal company. To make the deal more enticing, he added wine-tasting glasses and provided tasting samples of some of the wine. This way, at worst he came away with $7.50 per person, and perhaps more if they liked the wine enough to purchase a bottle. In the end, Michael had such a good response that he had to start scheduling tours on weekends to accommodate the crowds.

The problem that Michael encountered was that his staff was not fully updated on the new value proposition. Tours, once free, were now at a cost, and when people came in with vouchers there was some confusion since Michael was out of town when the deal first launched. "I wasn't there to help steward my employees to understand what was changing, how it was going to change, and how it was going to impact them, so the first week it went horribly," explains Michael. Once he returned, everything was immediately straightened out and the deal proceeded to be a major success.

Michael also finds it interesting that many people who use Groupon, LivingSocial, or other daily deal websites often want to get even more than that which is offered. "Someone will come in after the deal and ask, 'Can I buy ten more of these and can I get them at the deal price?' You have to be very careful not to shoot yourself in the foot. The problem is that you're sabotaging the business partner that helped you do so well in the first place," explains Michael regarding extending deals beyond that which you are offering through the daily deal site.

In the end, Moonlight Meadery saw $120,000 in sales, of which 80 percent was profit. They used a new value proposition to serve as a deal. This opens up another avenue of consideration for daily deal business owners or even couponers: finding a value proposition for a merchant where there could, and should, be one.

Today, Moonlight Meadery produces nearly 60 different meads, with a complex range of flavors including dry, semi-sweet, and sweet. The honey wines of Moonlight Meadery are now available in 20 states. According to Michael, they will run more daily deals having had such a positive experience.

Westchester Ballroom in Mount Kisco (Westchester), New York

A former nurse turned dancer turned business owner, Barbara Antes opened the Westchester Ballroom dance studio in Pleasantville, New York, where she and her instructors taught private and group ballroom dance classes for more than a decade. But when rent hikes made it difficult for the studio to continue, she picked up and moved a few miles north to the town of Mount Kisco, a hub of Northern Westchester, just under one hour north of Manhattan.

The new, larger location presented her with ample space. Not only could the ballroom hold both private and group classes, but could also accommodate parties and benefits for local charities. The only drawback was that she was not on a main street and needed to spread the word beyond her loyal patrons from Pleasantville.

"When they called me [from a major daily deal site] and offered to advertise my business on their site and in their emails, which go out to several hundred thousand people, I figured why not? If nothing else, the advertising alone is worthwhile."

Antes worked out a 50-percent split with the sales rep and offered a 50-percent deal for members to take a specified number of group or private lessons, with the stipulation that they be used in a single month. "I didn't want people strolling in for a lesson every few months. It would be very hard to keep tabs on who was who," explains Antes, who was also hoping that new customers would enjoy the lessons so much that they would sign up for more at regular prices. With the deal in place, each lesson that would normally cost $70 was now costing customers $35, of which she was getting half. Ironically, the $70 rate was already less than half of the cost of one lesson at the nearest "big name" high-cost competitor.

"It seemed like a great deal since I didn't have to pay anything upfront and it drew in more students," notes Antes. "I wasn't completely satisfied with the copy, but I figured their PR department must know what they're doing since they do this all the time."

In the end, Westchester Ballroom got about 65 new customers, of which about 10 percent turned into regulars. "[The daily deal site] sent the money in three payments, and everybody stuck to the rules," says Antes, adding that she would do it again.

The Ballroom continues growing in membership with a busy schedule of group and individual lessons. As for Barbara Antes, she's become a daily deal user ever since. "They send me emails and I buy gifts for other people," she adds with a laugh.

Witch City Segway Tours in Salem, Massachusetts

What better way to tour the "witchy" city of Salem than on a Segway? That was the thinking behind the tour business started by Jeff Langone in 2010. Led by friendly and experienced tour guides, visitors to Salem get to ride the state-of-the art Segways and check out the famous and infamous sites that put the city on the map more than 300 years ago, when witch hunts were in vogue.

More recently, in an age in which daily deals are in vogue, Langone decided it was time to sign up with a major deal company to run a deal on the tours. "We've done this deal twice over the past two years," says Jeff, noting that the experience was better the second year than the first. "We're open for business between April and Halloween, but our biggest business kicks in during June. The first year we had the deals running during the height of our season, which was a mistake because we had a lot of the daily deal customers booking and blocking out the full-paying customers. The second year, we decided to run the deal only between April and June so we could capitalize on the added business during the quieter time, and then fill our schedule during the peak months," explains Langone. It was also after the first deal that Langone worked with the deal company to receive a better split then the typical 50-50.

"One thing we also realized was that people were tipping based on the lower rate— if at all—which wasn't good for our tour guides," adds Langone, who now tries harder to encourage customers to please tip their tour guides.

Langone also notes that the sales rep was helpful, following up on how the deal was working out for the company. "We also decided to offer the option of purchasing a tour for six people at a 55-percent savings," adds Langone, who also recommends that people be aware of the maximum that they can accommodate since businesses can get a tremendous bump in potential customers and have to be able to accommodate them.

"You'll also see a lot of people suddenly realize they didn't use the coupon and you may have a lot of people showing up at the last minute," warns Langone, reminding people to include the phrase "depends on availability."

Now in their third year, Witch City Segway Tours have become the trendy new way to check out the city's highlights, while enjoying the benefits of daily deals as a means of drawing more customers each year.

FotoCabina
in Orange County, California

It has become more and more fashionable to have photo booths available at weddings or other major parties or personal events. One company supplying such upscale photo booths is FotoCabina. Brent Dedmon, who started the business in 2007, has since worked with a few daily deal sites to offer half-price deals on the photo booth rentals.

"We worked with the sales reps about three or four weeks in advance to set up the deal and discussed what we wanted to do," says Dedmon. "We offer a full four-hour photo booth rental, which includes service, delivery, onsite attendant, booth usage, print TV images, props, online photo hosting—the whole nine yards. It typically costs $1,500 to $2,000 to rent, and we were offering it at $699, which was a really good deal as far as we're concerned," explains Dedmon, adding that most of their customers are brides (about 55 to 60 percent), but that they also handle corporate events, bar mitzvahs, and other types of parties.

As far as working with the deal company, Dedmon realized that a 50-50 split would not be profitable, so he sat down and negotiated a better arrangement. Otherwise, he was happy with the results and the dashboard that the sites provided to manage the deal and see the numbers of sales. He also highly recommends keeping track of the numbers. "Merchants have to know what they are getting into and be prepared to handle the influx. It's a great thing, but, like us, you may realize that there are only two of you in the office,

> **Tip...**
>
> **Smart Tip**
>
> Daily deals are hot, and it's very likely that you are not the first to talk with a merchant about such deals. Find out what they did and did not like from their previous deal experiences and offer them additional personalized assistance to make sure those negatives do not occur again.

which can be a problem when you have 140 voice mails and it's only 8 A.M. I'd tell anyone starting a daily deal business to treat merchants as partners in this and help them prepare for it," suggests Dedmon.

The Flip Side

Sure, there are plenty of satisfied merchants whose businesses benefited from such deals, but there are also the negative stories of companies for which such deals, or coupon offers, have proven to be disastrous.

Businesses have actually gone out of business because of the deals they offered and their inability to manage the responses. One story tells of a popular hair salon that became a little too popular when 5,000 customers purchased a $99 half-day spa treatment in less than 24-hours. There was no way possible for the spa to provide the number of treatments and they were forced out of business. The owner blamed the daily deal site, explaining that the number of deals was supposed to reach a maximum of 1,300 but the site kept on selling them.

> **Beware!**
> As a daily deal site owner, you will want to be aware of and steer clear of a website called VoucherComplaints.org, which provides templates for consumers who are upset over daily deals gone wrong. They can get a crafted letter from the website to send to the deal site owners. Users fill in the blanks as they construct a letter that cites their state consumer laws that can be used to support their claims.

A house-cleaning service owner in Aspen complained that after he stopped running deals, which were not making him enough money to prove worthwhile, the deal company continued running the offers two more times without his approval. A dance studio owner also pointed out that she, too, had a deal run without her approval.

The cleaning-service owner also pointed out that chargebacks, including credit card charges, would also come out of the percentage he was owed and warns other merchants to look for such extra costs.

Hey, We Said One Per Person!

Another complaint about some deal sites is that they have allowed people to buy more than one voucher. For restaurant or storeowners looking to draw people in and turn them into regular customers, this can defeat the purpose. One store owner explained that a major daily deal site sold 640 vouchers to 440 people, meaning the one-per-customer limit was being ignored. The store owner explained that they lost over $750 on people using the vouchers more than once. When they tried to reach the daily deal company, they got no return calls and no satisfaction. This is where

▲

you can potentially challenge the big players by adhering closely to the contract and responding to your merchants' phone calls.

There have also been many reports of coupon users coming back with the same coupon again and again when there is a one-per-customer or one-per-family limit. Coupons need to be printed in such a manner from software on your website that limits them to printing the coupon only once. Merchants have complained about PDF files allowing multiple copies, and even photocopied coupons showing up at their stores. While you can't stop photocopying, you can remind your customers that it is illegal and that you do not support it—and make sure merchants are aware. Also sit down with merchants and review what counterfeit coupons (or fake vouchers) look like and warn them to be on the lookout for ones that you know are currently circulating.

While you cannot prevent the surge of bogus coupons out there, you can do everything in your power as a coupon site owner to keep such coupons off of your website. Know how and where to obtain coupons ethically and legally and do not accept coupons from "anywhere" as many coupon sites do.

Their Own Fault

Often, horrible merchants' experiences have been their own fault. Many merchants do recognize that there is no one to blame but themselves. A Chicago restaurant was forced to shut down after their attempt to draw regular customers failed. The losses experienced while bringing in one-time customers were too steep to handle.

An auto detail business in Oregon had a similar fate when they offered $12 worth of services for $6. After 600 people showed up, they were out thousands of dollars. In the end they were forced to shut down the business. Many business owners, unhappily, recognize that nobody forced them to run a daily deal with no cap or even put coupons onto a coupon site with a long lead time until expiration. These are the merchants that you, as a business owner, can consult to make sure the deal will be viable for them and meet their needs.

Learning from Others' Experiences

While many satisfied merchants smile happily into the night at their success through daily deal and coupon sites, others voice their displeasure on the internet. Stories of such "discount deals gone badly" are not very hard to find. You can learn from the mistakes of others and help your customers.

For example, the owner of Witch City Segway Tours learned not to run a deal during their peak season, while the owner of Moonlight Meadery, the honey wine seller, realized the importance of explaining the value proposition in advance to employees so that nobody is caught by surprise—he also figured out that the start of a deal was not the best time to take a vacation.

Among the other lessons you can pass along to your merchants are:

- *Consider the caps.* While it's great for you to sell 3,000 vouchers for a restaurant over the next 10 days, if they can only manage to accommodate 500 people over the next ten days, don't let them run themselves out of business. You want ongoing merchants and a good reputation. Help your merchants set caps or maximums.

- *Do the math.* You really do need some math skills to effectively run a deal or coupon business. Sure, you can punch in numbers on your calculator, but you need a sense of things like break-even points and markups so you can advise merchants. Hone your math skills.

- *Set the time frame.* This should be in writing and everyone should agree on when the deal or coupon should be posted and when it should end or expire.

- *Know the laws.* The laws surrounding giving away and/or selling alcohol are often the ones that catch business owners off guard, as was the case with one of the largest deal sites. Learn the laws about coupons (they cannot be sold or copied) and what types of deals and redemption time frames are legal in your sales region(s).

- *Be customer service savvy.* More customers equates to more questions and comments. It's advisable to win over customers and draw new ones, and to have a well-trained staff when it comes to customer service. This holds true for your merchants as well as for your business.

There are also some lessons that you should keep in mind for your own benefit, prior to meeting with merchants:

- Make sure you have everything you offer in writing and have legally crafted contracts (with some built-in flexibility) to avoid lawsuits, or at least minimize their occurrence. If you are successful, you may be dealing with hundreds or even thousands of merchants. You'll need to have the details of all such deals written down and saved in files. Saving hard copies is advisable.

- Be very careful that whomever you are dealing with is aboveboard and not breaking any laws. Also, if you feel that the merchant is selling legal, but low-quality products or services, you can politely decline to carry the coupon or set up the deal. Remember, you have a reputation to uphold.

- Try to help merchants find productive deals. Just as Moonlight Meadery found a value proposition in tours, you can assist in finding the best deal for business owners to run. But do not try to make a deal where one clearly does not exist. It's also important to be honest in what you put in print, on coupons, or on deal vouchers. Furthermore, do not let merchants pull bait-and-switch tactics whereby they conveniently run out of a product quickly and sell a higher-priced alternative, while accepting the same percentage-off coupon or voucher.

- Be careful not to expand your own business too fast. Yes, Groupon and LivingSocial took off and made megabucks quickly, but several hundred other daily deal and coupon sites did not. It generally takes time to build a successful business, especially as the industry gets more crowded and your coupons or deals are competing with many others. Set realistic goals and make excellent relationships with your merchants a priority. If they are happy and you are doing extensive marketing to prospective and current customers, your business should grow generically. Don't try to force it by expanding too soon.

- Get help! No, we don't mean see a shrink because you're crazy enough to go into this business—it can be profitable. What we do mean is that you should not try to do everything yourself. You will figure out early on that there are many aspects of this business and that you should be working from your strengths and getting others to help with areas in which you are not as proficient.

> **Tip...**
>
> **Smart Tip**
>
> If you need a copywriter, graphic designer, "tech guy," or all of the above, consider looking for students who need credits. There are numerous internships set up by high schools and colleges. Even without an internship program, you can find students who will work for modest rates to gain the experience to put on their resumes. Start by hiring them for short time periods (like two weeks) and see if all goes well. Many seniors are also looking for part-time work. And don't forget friends and family members who may help you out—for free or a modest fee—because they like you.

Summary Points

- You can become much more valuable to merchants by serving as a consultant and helping them formulate their deals.
- Whether it is a daily deal or a coupon, there are different phases when it comes to running a promotion. You can help merchants through planning, prepara-

tion, running, and analyzing their deal or even a coupon offer. Careful planning and preparation is necessary. From crunching the initial numbers to evaluating the success of the offer, you can guide them each step of the way.

- We used four stories of business owners who ran daily deals and were satisfied with the results. They learned from their mistakes and had good experiences. We then looked at the flip side and reviewed some of the negative stories that have also become part of the industry, some because of the deal sites and others because merchants did not prepare for, or handle, the deal very judiciously.

- We discussed some of the lessons learned through merchant experiences, and finally went over some lessons to keep in mind when you're starting out, such as not to expand too quickly or try to do everything yourself.

Marketing

When the founders of NoMoreRack went on TV, on the *Martha Stewart Show*, they gave everyone in the studio audience $50 coupons. They were also seen by 8 million viewers, which helped them add many new visitors to their website and collect numerous new email addresses to which they could send their deals. The site features many deals on women's clothing and jewelry, plus scattered (but good) deals on electronics. Yes, there are many ways to promote and market your daily deal, coupon, or membership site even if you are not lucky enough to get on a major TV show.

In this chapter we will explore:

- Defining demographics
- New age of demographics
- Many methods of marketing
- Public relations
- Advertising

Defining Demographics

Before you can successfully market a business, you need a sense of your audience's demographics.

- Who will go to your site and/or read your emails?
- What is your target age group?
- Who are their friends?
- What are their interests?
- What are their spending habits?
- What will entice them to make a purchase?

These are just a few of the questions you'll want to answer when doing demographic research. For years, surveys, interviews, and focus groups were used to provide demographic research. You would find ways to ask questions that customers or potential customers, who were promised some type of incentive, would answer. You could then collect the results and review the data, forming trends based on their responses.

For many business owners these basics are significant enough to plan accordingly, especially if they are offering a reasonably broad selection. Many coupon sites serve an audience looking to cut down on household expenditures, especially when it comes

> **Bright Idea**
>
> One of the first things many business owners want to do when it comes to marketing is create demographic profiles of their audience. This enables them to target specific offers to those people who are more likely to be receptive. For example, a marketer for Abercrombie might target single, middle-class females age 18 to 21, going to college.

to grocery bills. This often falls under the jurisdiction of "moms," as evidenced by CouponMom.com, DealSeekingMom.com, MoneySavingMom.com, or several other sites with the word "moms" in them. "Moms," however, has a broad base. As a result, some coupon sites may try to narrow the focus down to moms with young children, moms of teenagers, etc. Depending on how broad your offers are, you will determine whether you need to narrow down the field or just reach out to all "mom" demographics.

Economically speaking, income data may not matter very much today, since coupons are now being used by a wider array of income earners than ever before. Once upon a time it was assumed that most coupon clippers were squeezed for money. Today, in some manner, almost everyone is squeezed for money, so demographic research shows that coupon users range from lower economic homes to wealthy households.

If, however, as suggested earlier, you are looking to carve a more defined niche, then you will want to carve a more defined target market. Therefore, if your site is strictly about green, all-natural products, you will want to determine the makeup of green buyers: Who are they and what products are they likely to purchase? The same holds true if your site is for outdoor sports enthusiasts and features anything from backpacks to mountain-climbing gear to vouchers for deep-sea fishing excursions.

But, other than surveys, interviews, and focus groups, how can you find out about your demographic audience? The internet! Even more specifically, social media.

The New Age of Demographics

As technology is ever changing, so are the means of gathering demographics. Social media is now a primary source used for exchanging information as well as for gathering data. It is from such data that you can market more effectively. People talk about what they like, dislike, buy, and don't buy. Yes, they share plenty of information in their profiles, on their wall, in their posts, their tweets, and through a host of other means. It is here, from social media, that a ton of marketing data can be routinely gathered.

Influencers

Today, the people who have a say in who buys what are called influencers; they are essentially social media leaders with large followings who have a lot to say and to whom many people listen. Many are credible, others are not.

The point is you can utilize influencers on one or more social media channels to your advantage. First, you want to reach these people using Google, Twitter search, Facebook, or another social media site. You can search with keywords that define your niche to see who comes up. You can also use social media tools such as Social Mention (socialmention.com), which will identify influencers on various social media platforms.

Influencers are frequently posting information of substance (not what they had for breakfast) and as a result have many followers. They can help you spread the word about your site if they like what you have to offer. In some ways, they are comparable to the online bouncers letting you into the inner circle, or not. You need to find them on social media and let them know what you are up to with the hope that they will share your terrific deals with their many friends.

Social Graphs

One of the most widely used means of gathering information is the social graph, which links people together by their like-minded friends. Under the assumption that friends have commonalities, the social graph allows marketers to use those similarities to market to a target group.

In essence, a social graph is a diagram that illustrates interconnections among people, groups, and organizations in a social network, such as Facebook. The public information is gathered within the computer and made available to marketers. For example, Facebook provides social graph information (i.e., friend relationships, shared content, and photo tags) through their Graph API page, which is found at http://developers.facebook.com/docs/reference/api/. Other websites, such as Twitter, Digg, and Zooomr also provide similar information.

You can get a good sampling through social graphs of contacts between people and their similarities. It was Facebook CEO Mark Zuckerberg who first used the term "social graph" in reference to the massive network of connections and relationships between site users. Zuckerberg claimed that "it's the reason Facebook works."

Interest Graph

Now that we've sold you on the social graph, which provides the data from social connections, here comes the interest graph. This graph leverages data that provides a better way of determining what users like. Since some of the connections on Facebook are old friends who simply remember each other but have very different interests, while others are acquaintances with whom people share a few general commonalities—like their kids go to school together—the interest graph makes it easier to develop a profile based on actual shared interests.

Culled from publicly available data, the interest graph links the groups people belong to, or similar comments made, for example, about fishing or boating or even couponing. Similar photos from ski trips or vacations in the Caribbean may be

Mobile Data

A company named nFluence Media has created a new deal-Board app designed to figure out what people like and dislike and steer them to their favorite products and services.

The app serves as an aggregator by collecting deals from a variety of daily deal sites and sending them to the targeted audience. To zero in on what a user would be interested in, the app first asks users to take about 30 seconds and respond to a list of brands and major retail stores that they do or do not use by pressing the up key (for like or use) or down key (for dislike or don't use). Based on these responses, a profile is created and deals are then offered based on that profile. So far, the app has been very much on target with their self-generated user profiles.

gathered as well as interests mentioned in profiles. In the end, shared interests get calculated and categorized. This is helpful if, for example, you are marketing a deal site that focuses on activities for singles. You can zero in on those people whose interests include singles events or singles vacations and who are not talking about their family outings. You can go further to see who are the winter sports enthusiasts and who prefer lying on the beach. You can then separate by age groups and market accordingly.

Of course, figuring out what all these graphs are trying to tell you can be a bit disconcerting at first. Places such as Swaylo (swaylo.com), purchased by Facebook, GraphEffect (grapheffect.com), or GraphDive (graphdive.com) can help provide a detailed analysis of social or interest graphs for those of us who need some guidance when looking at the unique results of such graphs. They are not always easy to decipher.

The idea is to use the graphs to better target your deals and to write copy that will draw the attention of your specific target market. But it's also important to see the buying habits of your target market. Remember, many people on Facebook will list a number of interests, but that doesn't necessarily mean they are spending money on them.

Relevance

Some people have interesting news to report on the social network, while many others will post a lot of meaningless day-to-day nonsense. Nonetheless, the more data available, the more specific the profiles will be of your ideal target customer. You can learn that Fred is 36 years old, married with children ages 8 and 10, has parents living

Know Your Generations!

Today, it's important that you know your generations so you can zero in on your target market. Sure, we all know the Baby Boomers, born between 1946 and 1964, but do you know which market you're going after? Are you focusing on Gen X, Y, or Z?

Yes, every generation has been classified by age group and given a letter. Generation X includes people born between 1965 and 1980. Generation Y ranges from 1980 to 1994, and Generation Z are those born between 1995 and 2005. Perhaps the next generation will have to start back at the beginning of the alphabet.

216 miles north, drives a 2009 dodge Caravan with over 40,000 miles, plays golf on Sundays at 7 A.M. April through September (weather permitting), married his third serious girlfriend, prefers boxers to briefs, also prefers ketchup to mustard on hot dogs, and had a Husky named Maurie when he was 12.

What have you learned from this? If you are selling golf equipment, he may be a customer. The point is that we are now able, through technology, to create detailed dossiers of anyone who spends time online—creepy, isn't it? More significantly, marketers waste an inordinate amount of time analyzing and trying to utilize irrelevant details. "Let's send Fred deals on trips to Alaska, because he had a husky over 20 years ago and that's where huskies are popular!" Yes, it's that kind of overanalysis that has a 55-year-old bald man getting discounts on Soft and Easy hairspray because five years ago he took his wife to see the musical *Hairspray* on Broadway.

The point is, gathering data can be valuable, but you need to find some relevance in the data you receive from the myriad of graphs out there. Get a reasonable idea of what your target market buys without trying to psychoanalyze them. If you have a general idea of their age and where they are in their lifecycle (new parents, parents of teens, buying first home, etc.), you can get an overall perspective of what they might be purchasing without having to know their favorite colors and means of birth control. Common-sense graphs are not yet available, but you can use some on your own to decipher information.

The time, energy, and dollars spent trying to pinpoint and predict an individual's every move proves to be cost ineffective, but it keeps the marketing solutions people in business. In short, don't overdo it.

Many Methods of Marketing

There are various means of reaching your target audience. The trick is to utilize both online and offline methods of drawing people to your website. Using keywords to market your business with services such as Google AdWords is one way, as mentioned under Search Engine Optimization in Chapter 6. Make sure to cash in any free Google AdWords or Yahoo! credits that you may have.

You can also run banner ads on websites or print ads in publications. The trick, however, is to find inexpensive ways to get the most bang for your buck, since advertising can add up.

Talk It Up

Join groups on LinkedIn or use Google Groups (groups.google.com) to find other discussions, and then start, or join in, a discussion. Do not blatantly promote, but join a relevant discussion and use your signature to promote your business (i.e., John Smith at PhoenixDiscountDeals.com). While coupon groups and daily deal groups may help you learn about your industry, these are not the places to promote since you'll be preaching to the choir. You can, however, learn a lot from taking part in LinkedIn groups such as Daily Deal Merchant, Daily Deal Industry, Coupons, or Coupons Big and Small.

For discussing and promoting your business in a subtle manner, you should look for interest groups that match your niche. Also make sure your business comes up in your profile.

Emails

The best way to reach your target market, as shown by the daily deal and coupon giants, is by using email. This is your inexpensive introduction to millions of possible buyers. You need to gather as many email addresses as you can through legitimate means, and email your coupons or daily deals, but not through spamming. This is why we discussed the importance of building up your subscriber base earlier. Using incentives offline, you'll want to

⚠ Beware!

Remember, when offering email deals, you need to make them very easy to obtain. Do not have a link that just dumps the recipient somewhere on your site and makes them have to look for the deal. This is a great way to kill your conversion rate. It should be simple to get the deal from your email, as well as go to your site if they wish to do so.

gather as many email addresses as possible. Utilizing your social and/or interest graphs, you can better pinpoint your target audience and craft emails to match their interests. Once you are ready to reach out to your email list, pull the most recent deals or coupons earmarked for your site and feature them prominently with an enticing headline. Use themes within your niche and send them out early in the day, especially if it is the first day of the deal or coupon.

Remember to promote forwarding the email to a friend. Yes, they could figure that out and do it on their own, but you want to make sure they think of it.

Also promote upcoming offers so they will be on the lookout for your next email. While some daily deal sites send 2, 3, or 90 emails a day, your customers may get turned off if you are overloading their inboxes every day, so try not to overdo it. One a day may be the best way to go. Also, try to set your business up with some major aggregators (like Yipit). They can also email their subscriber base with your offers, but you will have to share a cut of the deals with them.

As for the look of your emails, they should be similar to the look of your website. However, you want to feature a few hot deals and not overwhelm your recipients. If they feel overwhelmed, they will simply hit delete. Also try to keep your email deal descriptions concise and make the subject line simple, such as "Great Deals on Fall Getaways." Emails can be a major means of marketing your deals or coupons if done correctly—keep tabs on your conversion rate from your emails.

Twitter and Tweeting

Twitter is a free social networking and micro-blogging site that has become a favorite of many business owners. By going to Twitter.com and setting up an account you can get started. You should use your business name when creating the account. Then, by clicking on "Join the Conversation" you can begin sending tweets, which are 140-character messages, or updates. You can also read tweets from followers, which are people who are essentially your Twitter contacts. The best part about Twitter is that it is an interactive media tool that keeps you updated in the moment. It allows you to converse in brief tweets to let people know what is going on. While it's difficult to respond to every tweet, you'll want to interact with current subscribers' and potential subscribers' relevant conversations.

The toughest part is figuring out what you want to say and whom to say it to in 140 characters or less, but according to users, those 140 characters can make a huge difference in attracting people to your site and getting them to stay.

To start out, you first need to have a username that is easy to read and relates to the topic of your site or brand. You should also fill out all of the fields in your profile, which helps people find you when they search. And don't forget to have the URL for your site in your "bio" within your profile. Include a photo that relates to your website. Most of this also applies to Facebook and most of the other social media sites.

It is also important to make your Twitter page attractive and appealing. Don't try to oversell, but get the point across that you can help people save money. If people like your Twitter page, they will follow you, and the more followers, the more you can tweet to people interested in what you are doing. Of course your real objective is to get followers that subscribe to your site for deals or coupons.

Spreading the Word

Not unlike Facebook, spreading the word is a key part of Twitter. Therefore, if you tweet about great discounts to your followers and they tweet to their friends and followers, you are spreading the word far and wide. For this reason, it is to your advantage for you to get followers who like what you have to say, and with a topic like saving money, that shouldn't be all that difficult. Also start following people who are linked to the topic of your site. By searching topics and locations, you can find people in your area to follow.

In all social media, it's important not to just promote, but instead to join the conversations. Participating on social media platforms means not just trying to sell, but taking part in what is being discussed. Once you establish yourself as someone credible, people will pay greater attention to what you have to say and what you have to offer.

Sometimes, simply talking about a trend or new product (or service) in your area of expertise can build your reputation. But it's important that you be yourself and not try to be too scholarly, pushy, or condescending.

Once you establish yourself in social media conversations or discussions, or even

Beware!
If you are shamelessly promoting yourself in social media, or spamming, people will not be happy about it and you will lose your reputation faster than you've built it. It is important to be subtle, respectful, and not to blitz people. Remember, bad news and a bad reputation travel quickly. Also, don't overcontribute to a discussion in a group or Tweet endlessly, or people will stop following you.

start a thread (on Twitter you use hashtags (#) to label a new topic of conversation), you can mention your website and link to it. People are more comfortable following a link if they feel they know you. It's also a good idea to ask questions and learn from people with whom you are in contact.

Reminder Emails

You can also send reminder emails, such as: "Last Day to Save $80 on Snow Tires, Only 7 Pair Left." Additionally, if you've gathered some information about your customer, such as their birthday, you can send a birthday greeting with an additional 10 percent off if they act within the next 72 hours. Yes, the 10 percent will probably come from your percentage of the deal (unless the merchant agrees otherwise), but you keep the customer coming back. If they are subscribing to your site, which is what you want them to do, you can also send a thank-you email with some of your hottest deals. The idea is to use emails to keep your deals in front of your customers and to make impulse buying really easy.

Contests and Giveaways

If your merchants are having contests or giving away freebies in conjunction with a new product launch or the introduction of a new service, then you can also promote them on your site and/or in your emails. People are always interested in entering a contest, and if it drives more business to your site, why not include it? Of course, you want to keep people who enter a contest coming back again, so make sure entering the contest also means subscribing to your website.

Most people also like receiving freebies. If you run your own contests or offer some cost-effective giveaways, you can also draw more visitors. Promotional items from the traditional T-shirts, caps, and mouse pads to more creative niche-oriented goodies can also put your name out in the public.

Blogs

As mentioned earlier, you can also set up a blog for your own site, using WordPress (or a similar program). Spread the word all over the place about your blog and write about the niche market in which your site specializes. For example, if you feature coupons, many of which are for groceries, talk about getting the best deals at the supermarket, or perhaps about shopping with your kids.

Whatever works for your site should spill over into your blog. Also, use keywords in your blogs that are specific to your niche so that the blog will show up during searches. Promote the blog in social media and on other appropriate websites. Also, if you can land blogs or articles on other websites, it can benefit your business. There are also places like Business Info Guide that lets you contribute articles at: http://businessinfoguide.com/directory/contribute.

Online Directories

There are numerous online directories in which you can list your website. Links from key directories help you drive traffic to your site and will help you move up in the search rankings. Online directories include:

- Business Directory
- Business Seek Directory
- Canny Link Directory
- JoeAnt Directory
- Open Directory Project (DMOZ.org) (free)
- Starting Point Directory
- Yahoo! Directory

> **Smart Tip** *Tip...*
> Remind people to bookmark your site. This way they will see you listed in their bookmarks or on their favorites list and remember to return to your site more often. You can put a little bookmark tab on your homepage.

Some directories will charge you, while others are free. Some say they are "free" but charge you a "review fee," meaning they decide whether to list you or not—since you are paying for that service, they are not free. For a massive list of free directories visit Free Directory List at www.directorycritic.com/free-directory-list.html. Again, keep an eye out for fees. You may also find some niche directories or those that serve a geographic region. And don't forget about the online Yellow Pages at www.yp.com.

Spokespeople

People love celebrities, even local ones. If you can get someone to appear as a spokesperson in a short video on your site introducing new offers or promoting your site in any manner, it can help you draw traffic. Even a celebrity photo and a comment about your wonderful site, or a testimonial, or perhaps a writeup from or interview with someone of interest to your audience can help.

When Twitter started to lose some of its initial buzz, celebrities started tweeting and turned the social media giant around. People began following the stars. Look for someone your niche market would like to hear from or read. People on speaking tours, with new books out or with other reasons to be out marketing themselves, are good candidates. Of course, you need to have a relatively decent-sized subscription base to get their interest. Be careful to watch your budget.

Public Relations

Public relations is an important component of doing business successfully. Good public relations can accomplish three things:

1. It can put your company name out to people who may not otherwise have heard of you without you having to advertise.
2. It can keep people who are already your merchants and/or customers thinking fondly of you and thus create repeat business.
3. It can help you maintain your image and reputation when things go poorly.

The key to good public relations is to get information about what you are doing to the gatekeepers. These are content editors, online producers, magazine editors, TV or radio producers, and so on. Those who post articles, blogs, or news items on any form of media are the people to whom you'd like to get your latest newsworthy information. Just the fact that you are one of 700+ deal sites or 1,000+ coupon sites won't be newsworthy enough to land you the exposure you are seeking.

First, you need to do some research via the internet and even by making a few phone calls to figure out who is the decision-maker (gatekeeper) at whatever media outlet you are trying to reach. You also need to determine the best way of contacting them—most will say by email and many will also say without an attachment, meaning put the information in the body of the email.

Next, you need to send a short email press release to spark their attention. You can always hire someone to write a press release for you if you are not comfortable writing one yourself. Do not hire a PR agency, since they will want a retainer and charge you a fortune. Instead, hire a freelancer to do the job for much less money.

Of course, you can always take a crack at writing it yourself. If you Google "how to write a press release," you will find plenty of information.

Press releases should be no more than three or four paragraphs, and feature an attention-grabbing headline. First you'll want a lead paragraph that gets to the point of your information. Next, you should have a paragraph that provides the who, what, when, why, and where of your story, with some pertinent details. Another paragraph should be a "boilerplate," which is a short paragraph that you can reuse over and over again, describing your business, including when it was formed, your specialty or niche, and a few key facts or accomplishments. Finally, you need to make sure to include all contact information. Remember, shorter is better, since people are not willing to take much time reading anything anymore. Also, put something short and catchy in the subject area, including your business name. For example, the subject area could replicate the title if it's brief, such as "DealCrazy Featured in New Episode of *Glee*."

If you send press releases out to your media contacts once a month, you can keep your name in their minds. Look for interesting angles and newsworthy information that will make them want to write about your deal site.

For example, here are some newsy headlines:

- DavesDeals.com Is First to Offer Free Merchant Consulting Service
- New Site to Offer Coupons for Adult Toys
- Local Coupon Website Donates $10,000 to Children's Hospital
- Daily Site to Promote First Organic Car Made from Seaweed

The point is, wow them with your newsworthy information in the headline and write about it in a couple of *concise* paragraphs.

Sample of a first paragraph:

Dave's Deals is now offering merchants free consulting services to maximize the effectiveness of their daily deals. The goal is to help merchants avoid the mistakes others have made when posting deals. The service, starting September 22, is free for merchants who sign up to run a deal and includes a 30-minute overview of how to prepare the business for the influx of customers and how to monitor the process from beginning to end.

Typically, press releases are written in third person and are sent from your "press office" or public relations department. Keep in mind that no matter how interesting you feel your news is, press releases will often be deleted by editors and producers. However, the more you send with interesting potential stories, the better chance you have of someone writing about your latest news in one of their blogs, especially if your news is "right up their alley."

Sometimes tying into something going on in the news can be helpful, so pay attention to current events and popular trends. Also, make the story something that is newsworthy to their readers. Self-indulgence, like the people who post what they had for lunch on Facebook or LinkedIn, does not work for promoting a business. So, think about what will benefit the readers.

Public relations is a cost-effective way to spread the word about your business. You also gain greater credibility when others comment on, or write about, your business.

> **Tip...**
>
> **Smart Tip**
> With a little searching, you can find sites that list the top 10, 20, or 50 coupon or deal sites. Make sure they know about you—contact them with basic information and let your site speak for itself—in other words, don't hype yourself or they will get turned off.

Bad publicity can also result from being online. Look around for criticism and respond politely if you feel it is unwarranted. Don't chase down everyone who has something negative to say, but instead select those who are influencers or have some credibility and carefully explain your side and defend your business. Tact is very important.

In the case where you have generated significant bad publicity, such as a merchant blaming you publicly for putting him out of business, you can use public relations to put out positive stories on your company and explain your side of the story. Public relations can be used as "damage control," which means a way of mitigating such negative press. Plan your responses carefully and be both professional and, if necessary, apologetic about whatever went wrong.

Advertising

Banner ads are costly but can be effective if they are highly targeted toward your audience. This takes us back to gathering data on your potential customers from online sources and graphs like the social and interest ones. Other ads can be costly and may not reach your target market. For these reasons many businesses today are paying for keywords, as discussed earlier in the book, and working hard to build brand identity online.

If you are going to spend money, before paying for ads, consider hiring someone to help you with social media marketing. There are a lot of people out there, many who have grown up with social media and know it very well—start small and see what they can do. Make sure you check references and get some feedback before hiring someone to do your social marketing. It is a new field filled with people with good intentions but minimal results. There are, however, social media experts who can build a platform for you and establish you on the key social media sites. Look for someone who understands your needs, your niche, your target audience, and your geographic region.

Summary Points

- Demographics allow you to zero in on your target audience. You need to determine who your target buyers are and reach out to them. The more you can zero in on the right target market, the more cost effective your marketing campaign will be.

- Social and interest graphs are two ways in which social media can help you find your target customers. These graphs gather data about social compatibility and shared interests to help you get a better feel for your market. It's also important not to overvalue the results of these or other graphs. They can help you, but you should not try to psychoanalyze your prospective buyers because they all like the Dave Matthews Band.

- Marketing should be a combination of your online and offline efforts. You want to reach people through social media, in particular "influencers" who have numerous contacts and can help you spread the word about your business.

- Emails are very significant for your marketing efforts, as they let you send offers out quickly to numerous people for very little cost. You'll need to carefully craft your emails so that they resemble your website and are easy to read and to navigate.

- We mentioned some old marketing standard tactics, like contests and using spokespeople, if you can find them.

- We took a brief look at public relations, which lets you generate media attention without having to spend money.

- Last, we mentioned advertising, which can be banner ads or something as simple as promotional items or signs in merchants' windows. In an age of social marketing you may be better served spending those advertising dollars on hiring a social marketing expert who can successfully help you promote your deal or coupon business online. Just make sure they come highly recommended and know what they are doing.

Know Your Costs and Bookkeeping Basics

No, they're not the most exciting aspects of being an entrepreneur, but understanding the costs of doing business and how to manage your books are essential components of success. Profits are your goal, and managing your money effectively is the way you can reach that goal. In this chapter we will look at:

▲

- Startup costs
- Operating costs
- Bookkeeping basics

Startup Costs

This is one of those rare businesses that can be started for a bare minimum or for many thousands of dollars. Much of this will depend on how good you are at creating and building a website, and how much marketing you can accomplish on your own via social media and other generic means. If you can build a following and generate a subscriber base without incurring great expenses, you can launch a coupon or deal site (daily or membership) for a few thousand dollars at most.

The most significant areas for startup costs will be:

- Creating your website
- Subscriber acquisition
- Merchant acquisition
- Marketing
- Software
- Office equipment
- Phone expenses
- Payroll (if you hire employees or freelancers)
- Rent or a lease if you decide not to start off from home

There will also be licenses and fees for starting a business as well as typical administrative and miscellaneous costs. Let's look at some of these startup costs more closely.

Creating Your Website

Realistically you can create a website very inexpensively, but you don't want to because you need something that looks professional and can handle a great volume of traffic. On the opposite side of the coin, you can have a site built from scratch with a top designer and spend many thousands of dollars (five figures). You may do that down the road, but you don't have to when you are starting out. As mentioned earlier in the book, there are places that earn their keep creating daily deal sites, and there are coupon platforms that also allow you to build a site without great costs.

Using Daily Deal Builder as an example, they offer a complete platform, plus training, marketing materials, and support, for $997 to set up and then $49 per month. You can also spend $3,497 and be set for life with a self-hosted service installed on your own server.

Daily Deal Builder does not take a percentage of your sales, although some sites take a 10 to 20 percent commission on sales. Shop around and review the offers carefully. The best part about these kinds of ready-made platforms is that they typically provide training, easy-to-send emails, and other perks that would otherwise cost you more money.

Subscriber Acquisition

This one comes with two big variables, the first of which is market research. You can utilize online marketing solutions providers that gather interest graph, social graph, and other graph data and make heads or tails out of it for you. This is not particularly costly and can provide you with a target group to reach out to. Conversely, if you feel that you know your target market group well, you can zero in on prospective subscribers on your own.

Finding subscribers and accumulating a subscription list is more time consuming than it is costly. You need to use your creativity and build an email list through a combination of "working" social media sites and advertising on Google AdWords, Facebook Ads, etc. You'll also want to work offline to reach out to merchants, associations, clubs, the chamber of commerce, etc. Again, these are mostly inexpensive ways to spread the word.

Your other option is to buy mailing lists for a few hundred dollars and use them. The problem is that many mailing lists are dated, not directed at your target market group, or obtained through illegal or at least unethical means. While it is more time consuming, the best choice is to build your own organic subscription base. As mentioned in the previous chapter, zero in on influencers.

In the end, the startup cost could be $500 a month or $5,000, depending on how much you spend on ads, lists, and target marketing.

Merchant Acquisition

This will come after the previous steps are in place. The expenses here are the costs of being a salesperson and going out and selling your site to merchants. This can include the necessary paperwork, new clothes for meetings, business cards, graphics—whatever it takes to interest merchants in your site and your subscriber base once you have one. You can also reach out to merchants through emails, which won't cost you anything, or even by providing them with fliers, since most of your merchants are selling tangible goods and/or services from brick-and-mortar locations. Also, many merchants, such as restaurant owners, have little time to sit and go through their emails.

Depending on how aggressive you are, this could cost anywhere from $300 or $3,000 for your first several merchants. Again, this is a major variable depending largely on your methods of reaching out to, and following up with, merchants.

Software

You will need to have a program such as QuickBooks to handle your bookkeeping needs and a graphics program to help with designing your ads or coupons. The most important software program is one that can handle large numbers of emails. You need to make sure your emails reach their destination, which means getting past spam filters. You also want them to reach many subscribers quickly, since time is of the essence before deals or coupons are expired. Email programs designed to send to subscribers from places like Aweber, MailChimp, SendGrid, PostmarkApp, and CritSend, among others, can cost you $10 to $250 per month depending on the size of your subscriber base. For example, Mail Chimp lists prices (for domestic mailing) as follows:

Monthly price	$10	$15	$30	$50	$75	$150	$240
Subscribers	0–500	501–1,000	1,001–2,500	2,501–5,000	5,001–10,000	10,001–25,000	25,001–50,000
Send limit	Unlimited	Unlimited	Unlimited	Unlimited	Unlimited	Unlimited	Unlimited

Office Equipment

If, like many people, you are starting your business from home, you may have most of the equipment, such as a computer and printer, already on hand. You may want to purchase a second computer, which will be dedicated to running the business. You will also, most likely, want to have the latest in mobile technology. Don't worry about bells and whistles. Instead, concern yourself with having mobile access to your merchants and subscribers at all times.

Smart Tip
Remember to have business cards, letterhead stationery, and a logo all included in your startup expenses. You may need to hire someone to design your logo. Include that cost as well, and make sure it represents what your coupon or deal site is all about.

Beyond the computer setup and software, there is not a lot of office equipment required for coupon or daily deal websites, so these costs should be relatively low.

Phone Expenses

You will need a dedicated phone line for your business. Prices vary widely on the type of plans out there. Some will be packaged in with your internet and cable service. Having a business phone, rather than using your home phone number, allows you to promote one phone number, while not having to worry about personal calls interrupting you while you are talking with subscribers or merchants. You may even want to have separate numbers for subscribers and for merchants, with whom you may want to have longer conversations.

While you do not need many features, you should have conference calling available to talk with a copywriter, graphics designer, and merchant all at once if necessary. You will also want any feature that prevents you from missing calls—rather than interrupting a call with call waiting, you can have calls routed to your voice mail system or to someone else's phone if others are working with you.

While many people use only their cell phones, it's advisable to also have a landline. Cell phones need to be recharged and sometimes the batteries go completely dead. You can start out with an initial cost of less then $200.

Before setting up a business phone system, you should:

1. Estimate your minute usage.
2. Decide how many lines or extensions you will need. Even if you are a solo act, it's good to have a couple of extensions for growth.
3. Consider internet phone service. Voice over internet protocol (VoIP) is a system whereby you use the internet for your phone service. It can be advantageous because you do not incur surcharges beyond what you pay for internet access. Sound quality can also be better. Cool Talk and NetMeeting are among two of the leading players that come with web browsers. There are also other companies providing such service. The downside is that if you lose your internet connection, you lose your phone service as well.

Payroll

Part-timers or full-timers can help you reach out to merchants and/or build your subscriber base. Thus, payroll expenses will be part of your startup costs. It's hard to find enough hours in the day to build up your subscriber list and your merchant list. This may necessitate finding some help. Obviously part-time help will be the less costly option. Consider the going hourly rate in your geographic location for sales help and train accordingly based on your needs. Estimate how much time you will need to have employees. For example, at $20 per hour, you can hire someone (or a couple of people) for 400 hours and spend $8,000 to help build a significant subscriber list as well as reach out to merchants.

> ## Beware!
> Be careful when offering employee commissions. There are headaches involved, as you need to keep tabs on how much income is coming in from the merchants that they signed up. You can offer incentives, which are one-time payments and easier to keep track of.

Legal and Accounting

You will want to have lawyers review the agreements you create to work with merchants, your online privacy policy, affiliate agreements you receive if you choose to work with an existing site such as Coupons.com, and any other significant paperwork or contracts. In addition, if you start an LLC or partnership, or you incorporate, you will want to have a lawyer on hand to guide you.

Accounting should also include a bookkeeper, which is typically not one and the same. An accountant should be there to help set up your books prior to hiring a bookkeeper to handle the ongoing books. He or she should also help you with financial decisions and, of course, handle your tax situation. A bookkeeper is working hands-on to maintain your daily income and expenses records.

You'll need to set aside a couple thousand dollars for legal and accounting to start your business. Bookkeeping will become an ongoing operating expense.

Additionally, don't forget to buy the necessary insurance. Review what you need with your insurance agent, since home policies typically do not cover business needs.

Administrative Expenses

Your contracts, your paperwork, and all of the small details that a business needs will add up. The paperless office is not yet a reality, especially when the IRS likes hard-copy backups to support your claims. Additionally, you will need to have hard copies of agreements for merchants to sign. Then there are all the little things from paper clips to pens, etc.

The "Sample Startup Costs Worksheet" on page 139 is a very rough estimate, since there are a number of reasons why most of these costs can be higher or lower. For example:

- If you become part of an affiliate program, you can save on subscription acquisition and/or merchant acquisition.

Sample Startup Costs Worksheet

Item	Cost
Website (domain name, site building, etc.)	$3,000
Subscription acquisition (ads, market research, etc.)	$5,000
Merchant acquisition	$2,000
Software programs	$1,500
Office equipment (new computer, etc.)	$2,500
Phone expenses (includes both landline and cell phone)	$500
Legal and accounting	$2,500
Payroll (part-timers to help built subscription lists or attract merchants)	$8,000
Insurance (extra for your business)	$800
Licenses	$200
Marketing	$4,500
Administrative	$ 500
Miscellaneous expenses	$2,000
Total	**$33,000**

- If you already have a large subscriber base, or a significant email list from some other source (such as owning a local newspaper or having another business), you can minimize your subscriber acquisition costs.

- If you already have inroads, and contacts, with a number of merchants, you can minimize your merchant acquisition costs.

- Marketing expenses are often estimated at about 15 percent of your budget. This can come down if you are particularly astute at using social media for marketing purposes.

- If you have any, or all, of the above you might minimize or eliminate your payroll costs. If you have friends or family who are able to pitch in, you can also minimize such costs.

- If you have a lawyer and/or accountant in the family or as your closest friends, you can minimize your legal and accounting costs.

The point is that you can start this type of business for less than $10,000 or close to $100,000, depending on what you have already that you can utilize and how big you want to be when you hit the ground running. There are work-at-home daily deal and coupon site owners who handle everything by themselves, have subscriber lists of roughly 5,000 people, and are making money because they are ensconced in a niche, which is sometimes simply becoming known as the local leader in bringing discounts to a town or a region. Some have started for a few thousand dollars spent primarily in building and promoting their websites.

Operating Costs

Along with the costs of starting up, you'll also need to figure out your operating costs prior to opening your business or launching your website. These costs are those that are necessary to run your business on a daily basis. Some of these costs are fixed from month to month, such as your rent, if you are working from an office, and your web hosting payments. Others will vary, such as your marketing costs.

It is advisable that you determine one full year of operational costs, estimating the variable costs and including the fixed costs on a monthly basis. Since advertising and marketing can vary significantly, you may need to adjust once you get started. Employee salaries can be your biggest expense. So, estimate what your needs will be and budget accordingly. Some operating expenses, such as your accountant or your insurance payments, may only appear twice a year, so you may want to amortize, which means factoring in these as monthly costs by taking the total and dividing by 12. This

Startup Costs Worksheet

Use the following chart to list your own startup costs. Hint: Fill this out in pencil because you will want to make changes.

Item	Cost
Website	$
Subscription acquisition	$
Merchant acquisition	$
Software programs	$
Office equipment	$
Phone expenses	$
Legal and accounting	$
Payroll	$
Insurance	$
Licenses	$
Marketing	$
Administrative	$
Miscellaneous expenses	$
Total	$

will help give you a set monthly operating cost. For example, if you work with your accountant twice a year for $1,200, write down $100 per month.

Bringing Down Operational Costs

Before you start spending money, it's a good idea to figure out how to save it—after all, you are in the business of helping others save money. So why not do it yourself?

The best way to save money in business is to do a lot of preliminary research and learn as much as you can about how the industry operates. Read everything you can find, positive and negative, about the coupon and deal industry. LinkedIn, as mentioned earlier, has groups devoted to both, where you can learn from the discussions, the postings, and the links to articles. Also, by searching on Google, or any other search engine, you can get the latest articles about the industry. You can also go to Amazon or the library (or the reference listings in the back of this book) and find additional books on the subjects. Too many people do not immerse themselves in their industry before jumping into it. They spend money needlessly and regret it later. You'll want to learn both the nuances and the most up-to-date costs associated with your industry.

As for saving money: Do things at the right time. What does that mean? Simply, don't hire people until you need to, don't expand before you need to, don't advertise and market your website until it's ready. Timing is also very important in business and many business owners waste money because of bad timing.

You can also save money by purchasing the previous model. For example, if the latest and greatest smartphone known to mankind just came out and costs $1,600, you can probably get the previous version for $400. In most cases it will serve your needs. And the one you would spend $1,600 to purchase will be outdated in a few months, anyway.

Basic Bookkeeping

Bookkeeping is a means of keeping track of all of your business transactions. The idea is to know exactly what you are spending, what you are earning, how much is owed to you, and how much you owe to others. If handled correctly, your books should tell an accurate financial story of your business.

Your bookkeeping process should include:

- Keeping records, and receipts, of all your expenses, including your payroll, marketing, ongoing operating expenses, and paying your merchants if you are running a daily (or membership) deal business.

- Keeping track of your income. This may include: income from the sale of deals; your commission from coupons used from your site or from affiliates; and/or membership fees if you have them. Additional income from other sources also needs to be included.

- Utilizing the expense and income data to see where you stand and how your business is doing financially

Smart Tip

Get into the habit of saving all receipts for business. This will allow you to keep a grasp on your spending and help when paying taxes and seeking out business deductions. Receipts will also be vital should you be audited.

To maintain your books you will need to use a ledger, which you can easily find through one of many computer software programs. In the early days of your business you will probably do fine with one of QuickBooks or SAGE 50 Accounting's excellent programs for small businesses. For those using mobile technology, you may opt for a cloud-based accounting software package like Easy Books or Kashoo.

It's advised **not** to put bookkeeping off, even if you find it boring. The more your business grows and subscribers are utilizing your coupons and/or deals, the more you will need to keep your income and expenses up-to-date. This is especially true as your merchants increase and your payments to them also increase.

Two Methods of Bookkeeping

You'll find that there are two methods of bookkeeping: single-entry and double-entry. Single-entry bookkeeping is very simple and is typically the way in which you handle your checkbook. A double-entry system, more commonly used in business, lets you follow credits in one account and debits in the other. Each account has two columns and each transaction is located in two accounts. Entries are made for each transaction in both accounts, one in the debit account and one in the credit account. For example, each time you pay a merchant, you increase your "merchant" category (expense) by recording a debit transaction, and decrease your cash (asset) by recording a credit transaction. If a merchant pays you a commission from coupons used from your site, you increase cash (assets) by recording a debit transaction, and increase "commissions earned" (income) by recording a credit transaction.

Double-entry bookkeeping lets you see your current assets and liabilities. It also makes it easier to create a profit and loss statement.

If you are not familiar with bookkeeping from past experience, you are best served getting some help, at least to get started or learn the software programs. Take a course, online or elsewhere, pay for some "tutoring," or ask someone you know and trust to

▲

help you get started. Unless you know you have the time and ability to handle the task, hire a bookkeeper; it will be well worth it. Make sure to watch over them carefully. You should also have an accountant from day one, who may also recommend someone to come in and help you with your books.

> **Bright Idea**
>
> The most important reports generated by small-business owners, for their own use and that of backers and the IRS, are a cash flow analysis, a profit and loss forecast, and a balance sheet. QuickBooks, and other small-business software, can help you put these together so you can review exactly where you stand financially. You'll be able to see if cash is coming in quickly enough to cover upcoming expenditures, when you may be able to see a profit, and if you are balancing your debits and credits so that you are not falling into debt.

Summary Points

- One of the first steps to starting a business, any business, is listing your startup costs. Since rates will vary depending on the size and scope of your business plus your overhead, you will want to carefully consider what you will need financially to start your business. It's recommended that you start small and grow your business accordingly.

- Operating costs, which are the ongoing costs of maintaining the business, include all of the ongoing costs that you will have on a regular or semi-regular basis. Again, you can estimate these based on the size and scope of your business. You'll also want to consider the going rates for rent and utilities in your area of business. Operating costs can give you an idea of how much money you will need to have on hand at any given time.

- In both cases, while starting up the business as well as operating it, there are wide parameters. Some people start up and operate on a very low budget, while others spent exorbitant sums over years to launch the business and have high overheads while running it. Again, it is recommended that you don't start off too big.

- Bookkeeping is essential to any business. No, you do not need to have an elaborate bookkeeping program, just one that will help you keep tabs on your expenses and your income on a regular basis. It is advantageous to seek out help with your bookkeeping, and you should hire an accountant to provide an overview of your financial picture and make sure you get started on the right foot and stay on track.

Finding Funding and Your Business Plan

Once you have done the math and determined roughly how much funding you will need to start your business and stay afloat for a year, you can begin pondering the age-old business question: Where's the money?

In this chapter we will look at some options for finding startup money. We will look at:

- Finding funding
- Business plans

Prior to finding funding, there are several steps you need to take. First, you need to know all of your financial requirements and have a good idea of what the expenses will be, as discussed in Chapter 9, "Know Your Costs and Bookkeeping Basics." Next, whether you are seeking funding from your grandmother, your friends, or a bank loan officer, you should have a business plan, or at least an abbreviated version of one that explains in plain English what you are planning to do with the money and why someone should take a risk on you as an investment. While business plans will be discussed a little later in the chapter, it's important to keep in mind the importance of having one, especially if you want to get investors to back your business.

Finding Funding

Sources for business funding include:

- Your personal savings
- Friends, neighbors, and relatives
- Your assets
- Bank loans or credit unions
- Outside investors (including angels and venture capitalists)

Your Personal Savings

If you have wanted to start your own business for some time, you may have been putting money away for such a venture. Now is the time to look at how much you have accrued and determine if it is enough to start a business on your own. If not, it may be enough to get you started with some outside help.

If you do not have money saved up specifically for starting a business, you can tap into your own savings, but not at the expense of your personal and/or family needs. You will have to look at your savings

> **Smart Tip** Tip...
>
> Startup businesses have a significantly greater chance of receiving outside funding if the owner has invested some of his or her own money in the business. This shows that you are ready, willing and able to take the risk yourself. After all, if you don't believe in your business enough to put some money up, then why should someone else?

after paying your mortgage, car payments, college tuition, and other priorities. Paying off your personal debts is also important before going into business. Plus, it will help when you are seeking a loan.

It is also recommended that you *do not* dip into retirement savings or borrow against your credit cards—especially in a shaky economy. It's also ill advised to borrow against your house. Savings used to start a business should be earmarked as such or money that you can afford to spend beyond paying off your debts and taking care of your family's needs.

The Friends and Family Plan

Be forewarned that relationships with friends and family members, even your spouse, can change once you are in business together, whether it is in a borrowing/lending situation or a partnership. The relationship can be strained once money becomes an issue. In fact, most marriage counselors will agree that the number one source of fighting between couples is money. As a result, you should make the process as businesslike as possible. This means that even if you don't have a formal business plan (and you should), that you can explain what the money will be used for and work out a schedule whereby you will pay your friends or family member(s) back. You should draw up an agreement, detailing the amount of money being lent and when it is to be repaid, perhaps with interest. Treat such a personal loan as you would treat a bank loan, and write out the terms that pertain to paying back the loan. In all instances, partnership agreements should also include who gets what if the family members, or friends, go separate ways. Make sure to spell everything out in advance so you don't end up playing the blame game.

 Beware!
Don't slice up the pie too many ways. Too many lenders, partners, or others involved financially in your company can become confusing (as well as meddlesome). Try to borrow from as few people as possible. Your days of selling to stockholders are down the road.

Any kind of successful partnership will require a delineation of responsibilities. If one person excels at sales while the other has experience in the technical aspects of the business, then you are all set. Such partnerships, in which each person meets a specific business need, are typically the most successful.

Many successful businesses are the result of spouses teaming up in some manner. You need to have the right personality combination for this to work, which means being open to hearing what each other has to say and compromising when necessary.

Your Assets

If you already own a business, you can sell it, or part of it, to generate capital for your new business. If you do not need the money for bailing yourself out of debt or for other immediate needs, this is a great way to finance your new business venture. One software developer sold his business to start his daily deal site. You may also have personal assets that you can part with to start up a new business, such as that antique car in your driveway or some old baseball cards worth $15,000.

Recently married couples have sold off one of their two homes once they began cohabitating, while others have rented out their old apartments to bring in money. Some empty nesters have downsized by selling their home and buying a slightly smaller one to make money available to finance a business. The sale of assets can bring you startup funding.

Bank Loans or Credit Unions

Banks, credit unions, and other lending institutions have long been the primary source for lending money to small businesses. If you are looking for business loans from commercial lenders, you need to have your financial matters in order. Commercial lenders want to know that you are not a bad risk.

A good credit rating is essential in order to demonstrate that you will be able to pay the loan back promptly. Before you start on your quest for money, it's a good idea to check on your credit score from the three major credit bureaus. This way you will know where you stand, should you be seeking a loan.

You'll also want to start paying off any and all outstanding debts. Then, once you reach a point where you have paid off debts, you can open a new credit card and make prompt payments or take out a small loan and pay it back on time, demonstrating your

Smart Tip

Tip...

Contact at least one of the big three credit bureaus for your credit scores.

Equifax: 1-800-685-1111, P.O. Box 740241, Atlanta, GA 30374; www.equifax.com

Experian: 1-888-397-3742, P.O. Box 2002, Allen, TX 75013, www.experian.com

TransUnion: 1-800-888-4213, P.O. Box 2000, Chester, PA 19022; www.transunion.com

Do this only once, since loan officers will also inquire and the more your credit ratings are checked, the more suspicious it may appear to lenders. Read your credit reports over *very carefully*, especially if your rating is not as good as you expected it to be. Credit bureaus make more mistakes than you would ever imagine. Make sure there are no errors on your credit reports. If there are errors, call the credit bureau to have them corrected.

> **⚠ Beware!**
>
> Never seek out places that can magically repair bad credit. Remember, anything that seems too good to be true is usually a major risk and you are very likely to find yourself in a worse situation than you were in before.

ability to stay on solid financial ground while building or rebuilding your credit score.

Several factors will come into play when it comes to obtaining a loan from a bank or a credit union. The economic climate, your track record in business, and your credit rating are most significant.

Lending institutions want to know that you are a sound credit risk. They also want to know exactly what your future plans are, beyond simply launching a coupon or daily deal site. This is why having a business plan, along with financial projections, is important. You need to show them that you have thought the financial portion of your plan through. Starting your site by utilizing an affiliate program can also help you build a business before seeking a loan to expand upon it. If you can finance the creation of the website on your own, or through loans from friends and family, you can show a track record of success through the affiliate program. Then it will become easier to borrow money to build or revamp the website and grow your own coupon or daily deal business.

If you are looking for a loan to start a business, you will also need to put up collateral for the loan. Carefully consider assets that you can use for collateral. Again, avoid putting your home on the line.

Crowd Funding

Crowd funding is a relatively new means of collective funding by which a new business (or an individual with a clever idea) posts their funding needs and people donate money if they believe in the business or artist's venture. Those who donate receive something in return for their support—much like you would give money to a PBS pledge drive and receive a gift. Crowd funding started several years ago primarily to help new rock bands fund their tours or recordings. However, it has grown to include numerous other pursuits, including new business ventures. WeFunder, CoFolio, StartupAddict, BelieversFund (for mobile apps), Fundstarter, and Quirky are among those sites that help fund new startup businesses.

One of the best places for information on starting and running a small business, as well as finding and securing loans, is the Small Business Administration (SBA) at www. sba.gov. Since 1953, the SBA has been helping entrepreneurs start, build, and run their small businesses.

Outside Investors
(Venture Capitalists and Angels)

The money you are seeking is considered venture capital, so the logical place to seek such funding would be from venture capitalists. The problem is, however, that most venture capitalists are seeking to benefit from investing in businesses with the potential for very large payoffs. They may also be looking for upwards of 25 percent on their investment, which is why most small businesses do not go this route.

If you have a unique idea that will transform the coupon or daily deal industry, especially from a technological aspect, you might try your luck with venture capitalists. Make sure you have a bulletproof business plan, meaning nothing is left out and everything is explained in great detail. Make it crystal clear how you/they will see profits in the not-too-distant future.

Angel investors can be a godsend, hence the name. Most are wealthy individuals interested in backing a business they believe in, and in some cases, have a passion for. Here, too, you need to have all your ducks in a row. Many people want to sit down with angel investors and get seed money to start a business, which is why they are very selective when it comes to whose projects they will back. While angels are not necessarily looking to make a killing, or even see money in the near future, angels are investors who want to be involved in projects they believe in and in which they see potential for growth.

If you are going to meet with a busy venture capitalist or an angel, you will first want to prepare an elevator pitch, which is where you present your idea in the time it would take to ride up or down in an elevator (about 30 seconds). The term likely won favor from the scene in the 1988 movie *Working Girl*, in which Melanie Griffith pitches her idea for the company in an elevator ride and wins over the "higher-ups." Essentially you need to present why your coupon or daily deal site will be a major success, what makes it different from other sites, and why you are the person for the job. No fluff, no hyperbol, just the key facts that make your business stand out in 30 seconds. Sell them quickly, with something simple and powerful that they can remember, and keep reiterating that message throughout your presentation.

Prior to any business meeting, you also want to look at your business and make sure you can answer any logical questions that they could possibly ask, such as:

- So, tell me what is unique about your business? What differentiates you from the competition? This is where you bring out your competitive edge, that which makes you different.

- What experience do you have that shows me that you can effectively run a coupon/daily deal/membership deal business? Here, you want to respond with your most significant and applicable skills for <u>this</u> business.

> **Smart Tip**
>
> Practice, practice, practice. They say it's the only way to play Carnegie Hall. It's also the only way to give a successful pitch—try it out on anyone who will listen. Get feedback for better or for worse and keep tightening it until there is nothing but the bare essentials. Then make it sing!

- Who else is on your team? What experience do they have? It's good to have a few people in place who bring expertise to the table. Even if they are not yet "officially" on your team, get them in place and present their backgrounds, stressing what they will bring to your business.

- How do you generate profits? Explain how you make money from coupons or deals, and how much you make. Include other possible means of revenue, such as membership or selling ad space.

- How large is your subscriber list? You should have these numbers available, and if your list has grown significantly over the last month or two, include the percentage of growth.

While getting your pitch in place and preparing to answer questions, a business plan can provide the written backup material that potential investors can take with them to get a better idea of what your business has to offer.

From the Other Side

According to surveys and interviews with venture capitalists and angels, they still see deal and coupon sites as viable, promising markets with growth potential. That's good news. But what are they looking for? Here are some notes from VCs.

- A deal site that can work in more than one geographic area, meaning it is "extendable"

- Entrepreneurs with the desire and ability to build the site into a larger business and keep up with rapid growth

- Not another Groupon or Coupons.com replica

- Strong leadership and a solid team

- Differentiation, something new with momentum

- New technology that gets deals/coupons in the hands of subscribers faster and easier, with a high conversion rate

Business Plan Basics

There are books, articles, websites, and software packages designed to guide you through the steps of putting together a business plan, complete with templates to follow so you need not recreate the wheel.

Business plans are typically broken up into several key sections in an effort to outline and explain each area of your business. It is a means of putting together all the pieces of what is a large puzzle—these are the individual components that start up a business.

Included in a typical business plan will be the following:

1. *Executive summary.* This is a short, broad, yet enticing summary of the business. What is the business all about and why are you so excited about it? Although it usually appears first, this part is often written last, after you've put all the pieces in place.

2. *Products and/or services.* Here you can discuss the types of coupons or deals that you offer as well as any other products or services. Explain their value and why your customers will want them.

3. *Industry analysis.* This is where you will paint a picture of the overall coupon and/or daily deal industry in which your business will be a player. By researching, and writing a few paragraphs, you will learn more about the industry in which you are about to embark. It also shows potential investors that you have done your homework.

4. *Competitive analysis.* This is a biggie. Do your research carefully and know who you are up against. Be realistic and list the strengths and weaknesses of the most direct competitors. Then, see if you can provide something such as more personalized offers or new technology that your competitors do not provide. This can be your competitive edge.

5. *Marketing and sales.* Now that you have plenty of details regarding what you will be offering, you need to explain how you will zero in on your target audience.

Tip...

Smart Tip

It's hard to find angel investors and/or venture capitalists. You might visit Funding Post (fundingpost.com), a business that arranges for special VC and angel showcases in various parts of the country. You can sign up and pay to attend such an event at which up-and-coming entrepreneurs, like yourself, get to meet with many angel investors and VCs in one place. Have your short elevator pitch ready and demonstrate the enthusiasm you have for your new business.

In this section, you will discuss your plans for marketing and promoting your business. This is where you define your plan of attack. If you are seeking funding, this is a very important section.

6. *Management.* A vital section in any business plan is management, where you will let readers know who is running the business. Potential investors will be particularly interested in this information, since they want to know to whom they are lending their money. Include all of the key people involved in making this business happen. If this is a solo venture, use a bio that features applicable experiences in your career, or personal life, that applies to this venture.

7. *Operations.* This is all about how you conduct business. Explain how your website works, including how customers find coupons or deals and redeem them, the type of arrangement you have with merchants, how often you pay them, what percentage you receive, and so on. Detail each way in which the business operates.

8. *Financial pages or forms.* The goal here is, with help from your accountant and/or financial planner, to make realistic projections based on researching similar businesses. This is where you show the math problems we demonstrated earlier and then project a year's worth of profits and/or losses. Then indicate how long it will take to start showing a profit. Also include a cash and balance sheet for a year to show a cash flow. Hint: Be conservative in your financial estimates.

9. *Financial requirement.* Very important; if you are seeking funding, this is where you include the amount of financing needed, based on the previous sections, to reach your goals. Again, be realistic. Research costs carefully and indicate how much money you anticipate putting into the business venture yourself.

Add to this supporting documentation, which will include various financial reports, and you will have a business plan. Do not try to dazzle prospective readers with hype. Instead, provide the real story of the business.

Of course, this is just a very basic outline. Before you sit down and start writing, you will want to look at other business plans in books or online to see the phrasing and style of such a business plan. If nothing else, researching each aspect of the plan will force you to start thinking about the many details that go into starting a business. That's when it gets exciting, and a little scary, as you see all of the pieces coming together.

If you need assistance, contact your local Small Business Development Center at sba.gov/sbdc or visit Amazon.com for books or software packages available that make writing a business plan a manageable task.

Summary Points

- There are a number of options when it comes to financing a business, including borrowing from friends and family, banks, credit unions, or looking for venture capitalists or angels to invest in your business. In some cases, you may be able to use your savings to get the business off the ground and then look for funding once you've shown how well the business can operate.

- If you are looking to raise capital from outside investors or lenders, you should have a brief, but well-planned, elevator pitch ready for possible investors. It has to wow them in roughly 30 seconds, so make sure you give them something that no other coupon or deal site can offer.

- We then discussed the importance of having a business plan. Included were the various sections that make up such plans. You'll also need to sit down with your accountant and make sure you have the financial forecasting documents that accompany a business plan, and illustrate how you will make money and how your investors will see profits. There are websites, software programs, and books available from which you can get the general idea of how to write a good business plan.

Selling or Closing Down the Business

Sure, it's a tad premature to consider selling a business that you haven't even launched, but why not take a quick look at what might be the full route of your journey. Once you have started, honed, and run your coupon or deal site for a while—even a short while—you may decide you want to move on.

In this chapter we look at:

- Merging
- The industry today
- Getting a proper valuation
- Selling
- Finding buyers
- Closing up

Merging

It's not unusual for small, niche websites to merge with bigger ones. In fact, in late 2011, according to data from Yipit, there were roughly 50 mergers and acquisitions of daily deal sites within the previous year. More recent statistics show that such a trend has not lessened. The bigger players in hot, relatively new, industries like to grow even bigger by swallowing up some of the smaller fish in the pond. This isn't necessarily a bad thing if you, as the little fish, have something the bigger fish want, like new technology, inroads into a niche market or area, or simply some sort of advantage.

This is how Savvi, discussed earlier, partnered with Access Development. Savvi brought their new apps to a company that was in the deal business for years and helped streamline the bigger fish to the advantage of both businesses. Savvi was not bought out, but became a lifeboat on the larger cruise ship, so to speak. And both sides sailed along happily.

Patrick Alubus, the CEO of Kgbdeals (a daily deal site), explained in a *San Francisco Times* article what some of the bigger players look for in the smaller companies, noting that they get calls often from businesses that want to be purchased or merged with the larger deal company. "We are actually being choosy, making sure their financials are worth acquiring. What is your functionality? You need to do more than your acquirer is doing. How active are your users? Do they open your emails? A high number of subscribers who are not active are not valuable. Also, we look at geography," explains Alubus in response to what he and Kgbdeals look for.

The Industry: The Bad News and the Good News

According to the reports from 2011 and into 2012, the number of daily deal sites being sold was increasing, while the valuation for such companies was dropping, due to the incredible growth of the industry.

On the flip side, deal sites keep appearing, as people want to save money, particularly while the economy takes time to recover. Venture capitalists and angel investors are still paying attention and larger companies are looking for the next big thing in the industry. As was the case with the internet boom of the late 1990s, and the flood of car companies way back in the early part of the 20th century, there will be some decrease in the sheer number of online deal and coupon companies out there, but the industry will keep on growing and spreading out with smaller, new niche sites catering to specific tastes.

And that's where you come in. But you need to be patient and let the other players rise and fall while you find the key to building your unique niche deal, or coupon, site.

Getting a Proper Valuation

If you are selling or looking to get acquired by a larger company, your brand, logo, subscriber base, and merchant agreements, along with your technology, are your primary assets. Typically, your profit margin will also factor into the value of your site. The higher the profit margin, the better the chance will be for a sale. However, in a business that depends largely on a subscriber list, another company may be more interested in such a list if it covers a niche market, knowing that they have the capabilities to better utilize the list.

Along with having a unique niche market and/or a high profit margin, having a strong keyword and search engine presence is a plus. You have a better chance of selling a site that comes up high on the search engines. How an online business ranks in the search engine universe is critical to driving traffic. Also, a high percentage of click-through to conversions means that your site is managing to get subscribers to use your coupons or deals.

Another factor in the salability of your company is how much have you have built up your following. If your website has a loyal following of visitors and shoppers, and you have built a unique sense of community, it is more valuable because it saves the buyer the time and money of having to build a large fan base. Additionally, the more you can offer that is unique, the more you can get for your business. In other words, if the buyer is getting something that he or she does not already offer or that would not be easy to replicate, then you are in a better position as a seller.

Selling

If you have decided that it is time to sell, you will want to gather all of your business records and financial data and prepare to sell the business. Selling a website is easier than selling a store or factory, because you do not need anyone to do physical inspections to make sure the roof doesn't leak or the vents do not need to be cleaned.

You need to sit down and carefully evaluate the strengths of the business, which are, as mentioned earlier: your merchant relationships, customer listings, and any unique technical aspects (or trademarks or patents) that you may own. Your brand or URL also factor into the equation.

What is your business worth? A valuation is nice to have on paper, but the real value is in what someone is willing to pay. You can read about recent sales of online businesses, particularly in the deal industry, to get a grasp of what such sites sell for. Like the housing market, this will vary based on the economic climate at the time and the popularity of the industry.

You have to assess your reasons for selling and how much the sale is worth to you. If you are selling to make enough money to buy a new home or pay for college tuition, then you need enough money to cover those specific costs. If you are selling because you simply want "out" of the business and have money saved from your earnings, you can

▲

Selling Tips

1. *Don't overprice your business.* Yes, you want to get a good deal and you can certainly bring your price down, but if you start too high you will scare buyers off.

2. *Be willing to finance a portion of the sale price.* The lack of available outside financing these days will often mean that you will have to do some financing to make the sale.

3. *Negotiate.* Whether it's price, terms, or structure of the deal, if you really want to sell, you may need to give up something to make a deal.

4. *Keep your records and information up to date.*

accept a lower offer. If this is your retirement money, you'll want to hold out for a high offer. Only you can determine what an acceptable price is to meet your needs.

You also want to think through selling from an emotional and personal perspective. Selling your business can be difficult if you are attached to it or it can be very easy if you are sick to death of it. Your reasons for selling will factor into your emotional reaction to selling a business. As a result they may also factor into your financial decisions.

Finding Buyers

If you have a business with a good valuation and are looking to sell, you can work with a broker, who will take a percentage, but may find better buyers. You can also advertise on places like BusinessesForSale.com or BizBuySell.com or on industry websites like DealNews.com. Another option is to contact the larger coupon or deal sites and see if they are interested in setting up a meeting. Make sure you have all of your financial data readily available. You must be fully transparent to prospective buyers.

Hopefully, you do not have:

- Any outstanding loans
- Back taxes owed

- Unsettled lawsuits
- Significant debt
- Complaints registered at the Better Business Bureau

You can also let other people in the industry know you are looking to sell through social media and in the LinkedIn groups such as those mentioned earlier, Daily Deal Industry and Daily Deal Merchants. Spreading the word via social media or by networking is a cost-effective way of letting people know you are selling your online business. And whatever you do, make sure you respond in short order to anyone interested in buying.

Closing Up

Of course, you can always simply shut down if you've had enough. Whether your coupon or deal business succeeded or not, if you simply do not want to take the time and make the effort to get everything in order to sell, you can simply close up shop. That's what is so wonderful about the virtual world. You can run your final deals, post your final coupons, and say farewell. Just make sure all deals are finished and all merchants receive their final checks. Tie up all loose ends before calling it quits.

So, What Have We Learned?

Hopefully in the preceding chapters you have gained an understanding of what it takes to start an online coupon or daily deal business. The industry is still going strong, but because of the popularity of such sites, you need to be different to succeed. You also need a passion for coupons and/or deals and to be prepared to spend an inordinate amount of time at your computer working on your business. One difference between a web business and a physical store, factory, or restaurant is that it's less "legwork." However, running a business, especially one in which coupons or deals will change all the time, means putting in a lot of hours.

We've talked about trying very hard to do everything aboveboard, especially in the coupon business where there are fraudulent coupons as well as illegal and unethical ways of obtaining coupons.

We also talked about the opportunity to serve your merchants as a consultant by helping them do what serves their businesses in the best manner. Remember, your merchants are your clients, and making them happy helps your business. And of course we discussed your subscribers, who are your customers, and how making them happy is the other significant aspect of your business.

If you immerse yourself in the industry, you can learn a lot, meet new people, enjoy what you are doing, and even make money. Like any business, you will certainly know in time whether or not this is the business for you. If it is, you can find new ways to grow the business and improve upon what you have started. If it's not, go back and reread this chapter about selling it, or simply call it quits.

If it turns out that this is a business that excites you and matches your personality and skills, coupon or deal sites can be very profitable, but as in any business, you will need some patience until it all clicks.

Summary Points

- Selling the business means getting your business records, especially financial ones, in order and making sure everything is up to date.
- You will want to get a valuation of your business that will factor in all of your assets, from merchant relationships to your URL. To get a higher valuation, it is important to have something that buyers want and cannot easily replicate. It is also important not to be in debt, owe back taxes, or have a bad reputation.
- Finding a buyer typically means looking for a broker, advertising the business, or networking.
- In a virtual world, you can simply end your coupons or deals, pay whomever you owe, and shut down.

Good luck, and may the savings be with you.

Appendix
Online Coupon and Daily Deal Resources

They say you can never be too rich or too thin. While those points could be argued, we believe you can never have too many resources. Therefore, we present for your consideration a wealth of sources for you to check into, check out, and harness for your own personal information blitz.

These sources are tidbits, ideas to get you started on your research. They are by no means the only sources out there, and they should not be taken as the "Ultimate Answer." We have done our research, but businesses tend to move, change, fold, and

▲

expand. As we have repeatedly stressed, do your homework. Get out and start investigating.

Books

8 Simple Steps to Internet Success: Your Step-by-Step Guide to Building an Online Business (Volume 1) by Jody Ortiz, CreateSpace Independent Publishing Platform, October, 2012

Cut Your Grocery Bill in Half with America's Cheapest Family: Includes So Many Innovative Strategies You Won't Have to Cut Coupons by Annette and Steve Economides, Thomas Nelson, September, 2010

Likeable Social Media: How to Delight Your Customers, Create an Irresistible Brand, and Be Generally Amazing on Facebook (And Other Social Networks) by Dave Kerpen, McGraw-Hill, June, 2011

The Six-Figure Second Income: How to Start and Grow a Successful Online Business Without Quitting Your Day Job by David Lindahl and Jonathan Rozek, Wiley, September, 2010

The Social Media Bible: Tactics, Tools, and Strategies for Business Success by Lon Safko, Wiley; May, 2012

Social Media for Business: 101 Ways to Grow Your Business Without Wasting Your Time by Susan Sweeney CA CSP HoF, and Randall Craig CFA MBA CMC, Maximum Press, August, 2010

Social Media for Business: The Small Business Guide to Online Marketing by Martin Brossman and Anora McGaha, Outer Banks Publishing Group, July, 2011

Starting an Online Business All-in-One for Dummies by Shannon Belew and Joel Elad, For Dummies Publishing, December, 2011

Web Analytics 2.0: The Art of Online Accountability and Science of Customer Centricity Avinash Kaushik, Sybex, October, 2009

Computer Shopping (and Peripherals)

www.Apple.com

www.Amazon.com

www.Bestbuy.com

www. Dell.com

www. Gateway.com

www.HP.com

www. Lenovo.com

Coupon and Daily Deal Associations

The Association of Coupon Professionals: couponpros.org

Coupon Information Corporation (CIC): couponinformationcenter.com.

Global Daily Deal Association: globaldailydealassociation.com

Performance Marketing Association: performancemarketingassociation.com

Coupon and Daily Deal
Website Building

Couponpress.com (affiliated with WordPress.com)

Coupontank.com

Dealcurrent.com

Dailydealbuilder.com

Dealcoop.com (Deal co-op)

Groupcommerce.com

Nimblecommerce.com

Oorjit.com

SecondStreet.com (Deadline Deals software)

Startagroupbuy.com

Coupon and Deal Affiliate Programs

8Moms.com

Brandcaster (from Coupons.com)

CentsOff.com

CityPerks.com

CJ.com (Commission Junction)

Clickbank.com

Coolsavings.com

Couponcabin.com

Couponqueen.com

Couponsurfer.com

Dailydealbuilder.com

Dealseekingmom.com

Everybodybuys.com

Formetocoupon.com

Groupon.com

Hip2save.com

Livingsocial.com

Logicalmedia.com

Makelifeeasy.com

Mommysavers.com

Mysavings.com

Netbates.com

Qdeals.com

Redplum.com

Savings.com

Savvi.com

Shareasale.com

Smartsource.com

Socialdealspot.com

Woot.com

Credit Bureaus

Equifax: 1-800-685-1111, P.O. Box 740241, Atlanta, GA 30374; www.equifax.com

Experian: 1-888-397-3742, P.O. Box 2002, Allen TX 75013; www.experian.com

TransUnion: 1-800-888-4213, P.O. Box 2000, Chester, PA 19022; www.transunion. com

Government Agencies
and Business Associations

United States Small Business Administration (SBA)
409 Third Street SW
Washington, DC 20416
(800) 827-5722
www.sba.org
The U.S. Small Business Administration provides new entrepreneurs and existing business owners with financial, technical, and management resources to start, operate, and grow a business. To find the local SBA office in your region, log on to www.sba.org/regions/states.html.

SBA Services and Products for Entrepreneurs
U.S. SBA Small Business Start-Up Kit, www.sba.gov/starting/indexstartup.html.
U.S. SBA Business Training Seminars and Courses, www.sba.gov/starting/indextraining.html.
U.S. SBA Business Plan: Road Map to Success, www.sba.gov/indexbusplans.html.
U.S. SBA Business Financing and Loan Program, www.sba.gov/financing

United States Patent and Trademark Office
600 Dulany Street
Alexandria, VA 22314
(571) 272-1000
www.uspto.gov/

Internal Revenue Service (IRS)
United States Department of the Treasury
1111 Constitution Avenue NW
Washington, DC 20224
(202) 622-5164
www.irs.ustreas.gov

U.S. Department of Labor
200 Constitution Avenue NW Room S-1032
Washington, DC 20210
(866) 4-USA-DOL
www.dol.gov

U.S. Chamber of Commerce
1615 H Street NW
Washington, DC 20062-2000
(202) 659-6000
www.uschamber.com

Host Servers

Above.com	Hostmonster.com
ATT-Webhosting.com	inMotion.com
Bluehost.com	Internettraffic.com
Brinkster.com	Networksolutions.com
Buydomains.com	Oneanddone.com
Cashparking.com	Register.com
DNSpod.net	Registrar-servers.com
Dreamhost.com	Reliablehosting.com
Dsreddirection.com	Singlehop.com
ENOM.com	Valuedomain.com
Fatcow.com	Websitewelcome.com
Greengeeks.com	Wildwestdomains.com
Hostgator.com	Yahoo.com

Keyword Advertising

Bing Keyword Research Tool: www.bing.com/toolbox/keywords

Google AdWords: www.adwords.google.com

Keyword Country: www.keywordcountry.com

Yahoo! Search Marketing: http//:advertisingcentral.yahoo.com/searchmarketing/en_SG

Office Supplies

Business Supply: business-supply.com

Discounted Office Supply: discountedofficesupply.com

Green Office Supplies: greenofficesupplies.com

Office Depot: officedepot.com

Office Max: officemax.com

Staples: staples.com

The Green Office: thegreenoffice.com

Other Websites

Analytics-magazine.com: Tech magazine about analytics and how they work

Couponintegrity.com: Promote integrity in the couponing industry

Dailydealmedia.com: News about the daily deal industry and tech industry

FundingPost.com: Seminars and information about business startup funding

Prologicredemption.com: Digital coupon industry progress

Software

Bookkeeping and Accounting

QuickBooks.com (bookkeeping and accounting)

Sage50Accounting.com (bookkeeping and accounting, formerly Peachtree)

▲

Creating and Marketing Coupons

Couponfusion.com (Creating coupons)

Couponpaq.com (Coupon marketing)

Email Software

Aweber

Constant Contact

Critsend

Mailchimp

SendGrid

PostmarkApp

Web Analytics

Crazyegg.com

Getclicky.com

Google.com/analytics

Havemint.com

Grapheffect.com

Graphdive.com

Springmetrics.com

Swaylo.com

Web.analytics.yahoo.com/

Glossary

Affiliate program: A program by which merchants or manufacturers reward business owners for sales generated and/or customers brought to their business.

Affinity groups: A group of people drawn together or united by the same interest or activity.

Aggregate sites (aka aggregators): Websites that receive and provide offerings of various other websites.

Analytics: The gathering and dissemination of data used to provide website viewing and buying patterns. Analytics are used to indicate visits to web pages, customer purchases, and demographic information.

Apps: Web applications (apps) are software programs that can run on a computer or other type of electronic device. They are most popular on smartphones.

Buy rate: Percentage of sales or "buys" from your overall subscriber list.

Competitive edge: The edge that your business has over your competitors, meaning what makes you stand out. This could be better customer service, better navigation on your website, more unique products or services, etc.

Conversion rates: The rate of visitors to your website, or to a web page, that converts to an action, typically buying something or joining the site.

Extreme couponers: People who engage in extreme couponing, which means making the act of finding and using coupons a major priority, and even going to extreme measures (such as dumpster diving) to find coupons. Some extreme couponers save thousands of dollars annually.

Host server: A computer that hosts one or many websites and makes them available over the internet to anyone connected.

Independent contractor: A self-employed individual who is hired by others to work for their businesses. He or she is not considered an employee of the businesses for which they work and is responsible for paying his or her own taxes. Independent contractors are also (typically) responsible for their own benefits, such as health insurance.

Influencers: A term used in social media that broadly (and sometimes vaguely) defines someone who has many followers and has been actively forwarding new information to a significant number of people through tweets, sharing, or other social media means of disseminating data.

Interest graphs: Data compiled on a graph from social media websites that groups users by their specific interests. Used primarily for demographic research prior to marketing efforts.

Keywords: Words or phrases that describe content on a website or page. They are used by online search engines to identify content on each page. Keywords can also be used as meta tags to describe and help search engines locate graphics, data, and text documents.

Loss leader: A product priced at, or below, cost to draw people into a store, or onto a website, with the hope that they will spend more money on other products sold at standardized (marked up) prices.

Niche website: A website catering to a specific area of interest or a specific location. Niche websites typically provide more detailed information, or specialized products or services, for a demographic group that are focused on the topic.

Operational costs: The ongoing weekly, monthly, and/or annual costs that it takes to operate the business.

Redemption: In the context of this book, it is the act of utilizing a coupon or voucher to receive a product or service at a discount price.

Search engine optimization (SEO): The process of using targeted keywords, among other technical approaches, to improve the ranking of a website by search engines.

Search ranking (aka search engine ranking): This refers to where in the rankings a website appears in the results of a search engine query.

Social graphs: Data compiled on a graph from social media websites that group users by their connections, and similarities, with other people. Used primarily for demographic research prior to marketing efforts.

Startup costs: These are the costs implicit to starting a business. While some may result in operational costs, these are essentially the one-time costs first spent to start the business.

Subscriber base: The number of subscribers, or members, you have signed up for your online business. The most important factor of having subscribers is acquiring their email address for marketing purposes.

Valuation: The amount of value attached to something, which can be a business. A business valuation measures, and includes, the value of both tangible and non-tangible goods and services.

Venture capital: Capital that has been invested in a new project, such as starting or expanding a business. Typically, venture capital is given to businesses with strong growth potential. There is usually an element of risk involved in venture capital investments.

Virtual office: An office that does not exist as one actual cohesive working unit but serves as such via technology, utilizing various people in various places to do the required tasks.

XML (extensible markup language): A set of commands by which there is a computer-to-computer delivery of coupons or coupon codes to your site from a manufacturer, or merchant, on a regular basis.

Index